THE FUTURENOW

OTIS PINNOCK

THE FUTURENOW
Copyright © Otis Pinnock 2020

Editor: Bettye Gilkes-Thomas
Cover Design: Joseph Opare

Scripture quotations unless noted are from the King James
Version(KJV)and New International Version (NIV)of the Bible

Dedication

Most importantly, I MUST thank my Heavenly Father for giving me the grace to write this book. He has seen me through some difficult times, but His love and care for me have been exemplary. He is the nicest Person I know and is continually revealing Himself and His Son to me in such profound ways.

Next, my beautiful family that God has blessed me so much with this endeavour. I have dedicated this book to you. To my wife, Donna and my children, Jaden, Ronel and Destiny; you all inspire me to be better. Hopefully, I am encouraging you to go for your dreams no matter what life throws at you. Without your love and support, I would not have been able to write this book.

To my parents, Donald Pinnock and Dorothy Malcolm, I wasn't the easiest son to raise. However, despite it all, both of you did your best to impart valuable life lessons to me. I wouldn't be the man I am today without your input. A huge shout-out to my Step parents, Sylvia Pinnock and Godfrey Malcolm. I am blessed to have two sets of mums and dads to share life with.

I would also like to recognise Ian and Samantha Roach, Neil and Jenny Douglas, Mildred Crout, Identry Ligon, Lucille and Fred Roach, Hervin Pinnock, Grandma Wright, Jennifer Cox, Leanna Rose, Pastor Joseph Boadu and CLF Greenwich, Sharon Stone, Empower Community Care Team, Joel Rueben and all others that have consistently supported my family and I. Your love and support saw me through the darkest of times, and this book is dedicated to you also.

Special mention to Pastor Jenny Clarke Singh and husband Paul, who opened their home and church (New Birth Tabernacle) to me. It was during this ministry visit in Canada, that birthed many of the concepts in the book.

To my family at-large, thank you as our shared experiences have provided vital truths conveyed in this publication.

To Bettye Gilkes Thomas, whose editing services were exemplary. Rachel Elliston, thanks for your input it really helped.

Lastly, I must give honour to those who have played significant roles in my development. Apostle Keith and Pastor Winnie Mcleod, this is where it all started and thanks immensely for your ministry, time and patience. May the Lord continually bless you with the fruit your service deserves and so much more. Big respect to Renny and Marina Mclean, Bishop Tudor Bismark, Bishop Hugh Smith; I know you all will recognise the truths in this book as it is a direct result of the truths you invested in me and so many others. Kim Clement, whom I have never met but whose ministry sustained me through the tough times. The timeless truths from Dr Myles Munroe that helped shape the objective of this book in becoming an influence for our King and His Kingdom are much appreciated.

Foreword

I have known Otis from his formative years. He carries a great anointing and operates in the spirit, in the office of a Prophet.

I therefore endorse his inaugural book 'The FUTURENOW". The writings created and penned by him will deeply engage, firmly challenge, encourage and provoke the reader to study the word of God, while explaining and setting patterns on how we should all live our 'FUTURENOW'

Apostle Dr. K.A. McLeod J.P.
Founder Miracle Christian Centre Int.

Introduction

I recall growing up in the 1970's and 80's. One of my favourite programmes was Star Trek. Gene Roddenberry masterfully addressed the issues of his time (the 60's) and set them with his vision of the future. These scenes sparked my love for science fiction that remains to this day. I would watch in awe at the gadgets Captain Kirk, Spock, and their team would use. Particularly the hand-held instruments that communicated with their Spaceship the 'Enterprise' as they continually explored new planets.

For those of us old enough to remember, there were no mobile phones as yet. The closest thing we had was a stationary public telephone box. I can recall the hospital bed that Dr McCoy used to treat his patients with the associated monitoring screen. If you are twenty-five years old or younger, you should stop laughing because the technology we are using today was nothing more than a pipe dream based on someone's vision of the future. My children are not impressed by the quality of special effects used back then, while they enthralled me. The point is, whether Mr Roddenberry meant it or not, by taking his story out of the current timeline, their team used creative imagination to 'see' and 'shape' the future.

When George Lucas wrote and directed his soap opera in the stars that became the box office phenomenon 'Star Wars'. He encountered limitations that then present-day technology could not solve. The special effects needed for the film were not sufficient to support his imagination, dream or vision. So, what did he do? He created technology with the future (his idea) in mind and, consequently, Industrial & Light & Magic was born. That special-effects company has since changed the cinematic experience forever and produced hundreds of films since its inception including E.T, Forrest Gump, Jurassic Park, Schindler's List and numerous others.

While showcasing historic game-changers who have experienced a sense of the future operating in their lives, we have Rev. Dr Martin Luther King, Jr, Marcus Garvey, Nelson Mandela, Steve Jobs, Bill Gates and many more. While this is not a new phenomenon, several great men and women of all races and ethnicities have shaped the present by having a glimpse of the future.

In my humble opinion, there is no other game-changer more significant than a young Jewish man whom I am proud to say has become my Lord and the One model of living that I follow. His name is Jesus Christ! His accomplishments caused such phenomenal change that time itself is measured by His lifetime! He modelled what I call a "FutureNow" lifestyle and shook up the foundations of the world! With all that is currently going on in today's society, we desperately need His lifestyle modelled and an army of planet shakers armed with insight into a glorious future.

Welcome to the "FutureNow"!

Contents

CHAPTER ONE

The Original Time Zone

HE Speaks...

> In the past, God spoke to our ancestors through the prophets
> at many times and in various ways, but in these last days he
> has spoken to us by his Son, whom he appointed heir of all
> things, and through whom also he made the universe. The
> Son is the radiance of God's glory and the exact
> representation of his being, sustaining all things by his
> powerful word. After he had provided purification for sins,
> he sat down at the right hand of the Majesty in heaven.
> **Hebrews 1:1-3**

From the beginning of time, Father has always demonstrated His
willingness to communicate His Person to us. From the Garden of
Eden until the present time, He has continuously revealed His heart
and His plans using a variety of methods. Prophecy, despite its
varied forms and manifestations, can be described as time-based
communication from a Being not limited to time, space or matter.
It is a vehicle through which Father shares His Heart and
continuously reveals Himself. The purpose of this book is to
reintroduce the prophetic and its role in enabling us to live a
kingdom-based lifestyle. This dimension (prophetic) has been
greatly misunderstood and has at times produced prophetic-based

behaviour that is not consistent with the character of the One we are all called to represent.

The scripture mentioned above indicates that God in these last days speaks to us through His Son. In Old Testament times, He spoke through individual prophets spanning thousands of years. Each with a different theme depending on the times they lived in but all having the distinct signature of Divine communication.

However, things have changed in the New Testament, according to the book of Ephesians, The Son (Christ) died, resurrected and ascended on high. He gave to the church what is commonly known as the 'ascension gifts'; the Apostle, Prophet, Evangelist, Teacher and Pastor. All of which are extensions of Himself and placed them in men **and** women. Their purpose is to make the body of Christ more Christ-like and to equip them to do the work of the ministry. In other words, to reveal the SON in each believer and to equip them all to operate in their SONSHIP. When you see an individual operating as a Pastor, for example, it is Christ **THE** Pastor operating through them. The same is true for an Apostle, Evangelist, Teacher or Prophet. Further investigation with His dealings throughout history, I see an interesting phenomenon. His communication via the prophetic is loaded with information pointing to the future. The language used is generally present-future or future-present; let me highlight an example.

> The LORD had said to Abram, "Go from your country, your people and your father's household to the land I will show you.
> "I will make you into a great nation,
> and I will bless you;
> I will make your name great,

and you will be a blessing[a]
I will bless those who bless you,
and whoever curses you I will curse;
and all peoples on earth
will be blessed through you."]
Genesis 12:1-3

In this discourse, verse one dealt with the present, while the following verses dealt with the future. A prophetic word that introduced Abram to "future now" living. During this interaction, Abram left the city of Harran (Turkey) with some insight into his future. He was approximately 75 years-old and childless at the time. He then left his extended family with his wife, nephew and servants and walked into the unknown. With the benefit of hindsight, we can now see that this was the beginnings of the nation of Israel.

What happened here? Basically, the Future was speaking. Once this happens, it tends to trouble our present. In Abram's case, it caused him to leave the surroundings he was used to and walk into the unfamiliar. This doesn't mean that his journey was easy and further study of his life in the book of Genesis will attest to this. However, insight into the future helped him stay the course and he is now rightly called the 'Father of Faith'. With all the uncertainty in our present times, we desperately need to see a group of people rise, armed with a certainty of the future. A remnant that will initiate transformation within our communities and nations.

Introducing the Original Time Zone

As previously discussed, prophecy reveals the Father's heart and mind and is future-layered information. This information has its source in the original time zone and not the one we currently live in and experience. Conventional time is usually measured by a variety of definitions (i.e. seconds, minutes, hours, day, weeks, months, years, decades, centuries and ages etc.) but for the purposes of this particular chapter, we will use the following categories of PAST, PRESENT and FUTURE. The past measures moments/events that have already been captured in time. The present is used in relation to time that is currently unfolding before us. The future relates to moments/events that are yet to come. It is generally understood that time is measured by the Earth's rotation around the Sun. One rotation takes approximately 365 days a year and depending on the Earth's angle and where you are situated, the seasons will be determined. Currently, I live in the northern hemisphere and am enjoying the summer season. However, in the Southern Hemisphere in places like Australia, they are experiencing winter. According to scriptures, the commodity known as "time" is not the original one. It was created or birthed from the original time zone. The creation account given in the book of beginnings shows us the origin of 'time' itself. As incredible as it sounds, our current slip of time has a beginning and will come to an end in a designated point in the future. Once this occurs, 'time' will again revert to and be enveloped within the original time zone. Let's take another look at the book of beginnings to discover more.

In the beginning God created the heavens and the earth.
Genesis 1:1

This verse alone gives us so much information. It describes an event taking place in the past long ago. That term 'beginning' can also mean 'in the dateless or timeless past'. It relates not only to an event but also to a time zone, the original one not measured in the conventional sense. Further reading in the creation account in Genesis 1 reveals that basis of time measurement as we know it was not created until the 'fourth day'. The sun, moon, stars and other planets in our solar system, were created **AFTER** this remarkable event. The word generally used to describe this 'timeless' zone or era is called Eternity. Astronauts, when finally breaking free from the Earth's gravitational pull, describe a sense of weightlessness and timelessness. When one dies, it is often said that the person has passed into Eternity, into a time zone which runs concurrently with our own. It is a zone where the laws that govern time have no effect and happens to be the time zone that God operates in. Time as we know it, past present **and** the future is housed or resides within Eternity. If that is true, then the future isn't just something waiting to materialise, it is something that already **EXISTS** waiting in our tomorrows.

CHAPTER TWO

Eternity Within

Praise be to the God and Father of our Lord Jesus Christ, who has blessed us in the heavenly realms with every spiritual blessing in Christ. For he chose us in him before the creation of the world to be holy and blameless in his sight. In love he[b] predestined us for adoption to sonship[c] through Jesus Christ, in accordance with his pleasure and will—to the praise of his glorious grace, which he has freely given us in the One he loves. In him we have redemption through his blood, the forgiveness of sins, in accordance with the riches of God's grace that he lavished on us. With all wisdom and understanding, he[d] made known to us the mystery of his will according to his good pleasure, which he purposed in Christ, to be put into effect when the times reach their fulfilment—to bring unity to all things in heaven and on earth under Christ.In him we were also chosen,[e] having been predestined according to the plan of him who works out everything in conformity with the purpose of his will.
Ephesians 1:3-11

No other portion of scripture in my humble opinion details the Father's interaction with time as much as this one. Eternity is the original time-zone, it is also the time zone of the invisible/spiritual realm and 'time' as we know it is 'housed' within it (Please refer to diagram 1 below). If we go back as far as we can, we reach Eternity; and if we are to do the same in the future, according to the scriptures, there is a point where time as we know it comes to an end. We are, at some point, between the beginning and the end of time itself. The Bible calls the times we live in as the 'Last Days'. More on that later.

Diagram 1

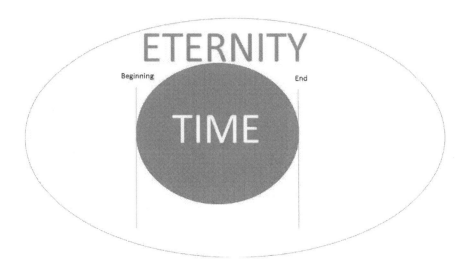

I will now use excerpts of the passage above with the following diagrams that outline the relevant time zones used. It will give us an initial understanding of how the Father interacts with Eternity and time.

Diagram 1 outlines both time zones, Father lives and resides in the outer circle of 'Eternity' but interacts acutely within the inner circle known as 'Time'.

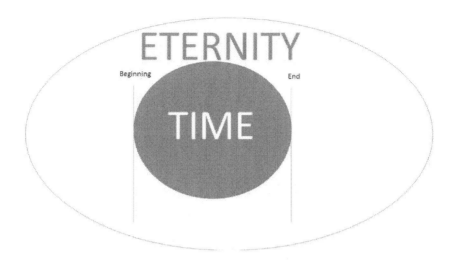

'For he chose us in him before the creation of the world to be holy and blameless in his sight. In love 5he[b] predestined us for adoption to sonship[c] through Jesus Christ, in accordance with his pleasure and will— 6to the praise of his glorious grace, which he has freely given us in the One he loves'

These verses let us know that Father chose and predestined us before creation to become SONS and DAUGHTERS, diagram 2 highlights 'when' this occurred.

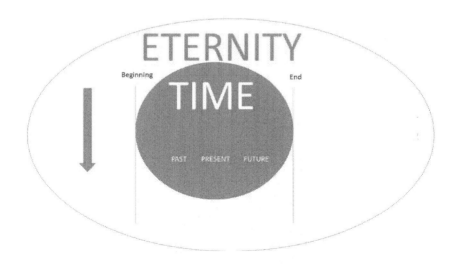

'In him we have redemption through his blood, the forgiveness of sins, in accordance with the riches of God's grace 8that he lavished on us. With all wisdom and understanding.'

This third diagram (3) relates to our present reality.

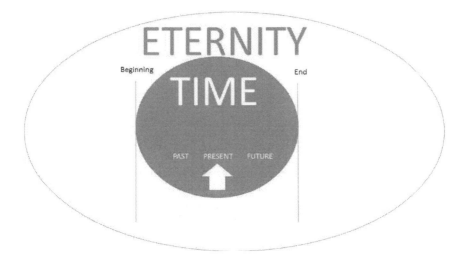

'he[d] made known to us the mystery of his will according to his good pleasure, which he purposed in Christ, to be put into effect when the times reach their fulfilment—to bring unity to all things in heaven and on earth under Christ'

The information above addresses the culmination of a series of events that are yet to come. (diagram 4)

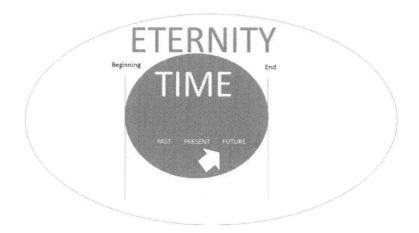

Eternity, itself has a past, present and future. It is the time zone of the invisible, the time zone of Heaven. It has seasons, days and continuous moments. It has always been the Father's desire to synchronise both time zones in order to get His Eternal plans and purposes for the Earth fulfilled.

The Bible, especially the New Testament makes it very clear that the Father made his plans before the creation of the world. Diagram 2 highlights this however since the dawn of time, He has been progressively revealing them to us. Not only, His plans but also His key times and seasons to synchronise both the time zones of Heaven and Earth.

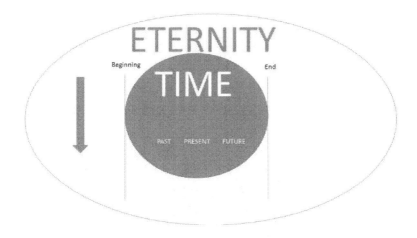

In order to synchronise both time zones, we are first introduced to the Jewish Calendar (not the Gregorian one we generally use today) which contain the Jewish feasts or holidays. This is a time system designed to integrate Eternity with time. The Jewish Calendar is mainly lunar, based on the moon's rotational cycle and does not last as long as the Gregorian one (360 days a year instead of 365 days). From what we understand from the Bible, Father operates in cycles of seven, be it seven days, seven weeks or even seven years etc. Most of the key Hebrew feasts operate using these cycles of seven.

The Feasts

The Lord said to Moses, "Speak to the Israelites and say to them: 'These are my appointed festivals, the appointed festivals of the Lord, which you are to proclaim as sacred assemblies.

Leviticus 23:1-2

After being delivered from Egypt and during the journey to the promised land, Abraham's descendants (Israel) received what is known as the 'Law' or Torah. Many instructions covering all aspects of life, civil life, governance, worship, finance, etc., were given. In this instance, Father introduces them to a series of celebrations called feasts that the Jewish people celebrate to this day. The Lord actually called the feasts, 'My appointed feasts', the Hoffman Christian Standard Bible translates the above this way.

"Speak to the Israelites and tell them: These are My appointed times, the times of the Lord that you will proclaim as sacred assemblies."

His appointed times and the 'times of the Lord' to proclaim are sacred assemblies. We generally and correctly use the term Jewish Feasts but Father declares them as His own at specific moments in the year when the time zones of Heaven and Earth synchronise. There are seven significant feasts/ festivals of the Lord and they are listed below.

Passover
Unleavened Bread
First Fruits
Pentecost
Trumpets
Day of Atonement
Tabernacles

Three out of the seven feasts occur in Spring, one in the summer and the others in Autumn. It is generally thought by scholars that the Spring and Summer feasts have already been fulfilled in Christ. Those in autumn speak prophetically to events in the future. I will now provide brief explanations of each and their own unique significance and relevance where Jesus is concerned.

Passover

Upon the final plague sent to Egypt, the Israeli's were commanded to kill a lamb and dab its blood upon their lintels and doorposts. They were also instructed to roast the lamb and have the very first Passover meal accompanied with unleavened bread and bitter herbs. Meanwhile, the angel of death was about to pass through the land with a mandate to kill the firstborn of every living thing, whether man or beast.

When the angel passed through and saw the lamb's blood, it would 'Pass Over' that house without fulfilling its mandate. This prophetic drama had to be observed annually not only to represent what happened at the time but also to point towards the future when the real Passover lamb would be slain; highlighting a plan hatched in Eternity waiting for the right 'time' to manifest on Earth. Jesus is known as the 'Lamb of God' and was crucified during the Passover celebrations. Closer scrutiny reveals that He was crucified at the same time that lambs were presented and killed during the celebrations.

Unleavened Bread

Immediately following Passover, the feast of unleavened bread begins. For seven days only unleavened (bread without yeast) was to be eaten. This was not only to serve as a reminder for future generations of what their ancestors went through upon their liberation from Egypt but also pointed to the future. Again, Father intertwines Eternity with time as we'll see with all of the feasts.

Unleavened bread is made without yeast, which generally correlates with sin in the Bible. Jesus was born in Bethlehem, which translates to 'the house of bread'. He is also known as' The Bread of Life' and before His trial, Jesus partook of the last supper, broke bread, drank wine and said, 'This is my body which is broken for you.' He lived a life without sin, died and was buried on the 1st day of this feast.

First Fruits

On the day after the Sabbath, following the feast of unleavened bread, there is the feast of first fruits. This feast is agricultural in nature and acknowledges the 'first fruits' or the first crops produced after the planting of seed. A lamb had to be sacrificed, and the crops waved before the Lord as an offering was given. The first crops emerging from the land was dedicated to the Lord. In fact, Jesus was raised from the dead during the appointed time of first fruits. When describing Jesus's resurrection the Apostle Paul says the following

> 'But Christ has indeed been raised from the dead, the first fruits of those who have fallen asleep. For since death came through a man, the resurrection of the dead comes also through a man. For as in Adam all die, so in Christ all will be made alive. But each in turn: Christ, the first fruits; then, when he comes, those who belong to him.'
> 1 Cor 15:21-23

The feast of first fruits also pointed to the future and symbolizes the resurrection of Jesus from the dead. Accordingly, Christ is symbolised as the first fruit of those who have- fallen asleep (the dead).

Pentecost

Fifty days following Passover, the feast of Pentecost is celebrated. This feast celebrates the wheat harvest. The Jews were instructed again to bring their 'first fruits' of the harvest to the Lord, along with yeast/grain baked bread, drink offerings and animal sacrifices. People would migrate from all over the land to present their offering to the Tabernacle or Temple depending on which era they lived in.

According to Jewish folklore, Moses presented the Torah on this day. Before and after Jesus died and was raised to life, He mentioned and talked about the coming Holy Spirit. He even instructed His followers to wait to be filled and empowered by the Holy Spirit. Hence, something unusual happened in Jerusalem two thousand years ago, which many scholars refer to as the 'birth' of the church. Luke's account in the book of Acts says the following;

'When the day of Pentecost came, they were all together in one place. Suddenly a sound like the blowing of a violent wind came from heaven and filled the whole house where they were sitting. They saw what seemed to be tongues of fire that separated and came to rest on each of them. All of them were filled with the Holy Spirit and began to speak in other tongues[a] as the Spirit enabled them.'
Acts 2:1-4

The Holy Spirit was released on the day of Pentecost. At the same time, Jews from around the known world would come and celebrate. With Jesus's death, burial and resurrection meeting Heaven's terms for obtaining our salvation, fifty days later, Father sealed the deal by sending the Holy Spirit. The Apostle Paul gives further insight.

'In him we were also chosen,[e] having been predestined according to the plan of him who works out everything in conformity with the purpose of his will, in order that we, who were the first to put our hope in Christ, might be for the praise of his glory. And you also were included in Christ when you heard the message of truth, the gospel of your salvation. When you believed, you were marked in him with a seal, the promised Holy Spirit, who is a deposit guaranteeing our inheritance until the redemption of those who are God's possession—to the praise of his glory.'
Ephesians 1:11-14

Feast of Trumpets

On the first day of the seventh month (the month of Tishri), trumpets are blown to signify the beginning of this feast. No work is to be done on this day and food offerings were presented before the Lord. The name of this feast has changed in recent times to Rosh Hashanah which celebrates the Jewish New Year.

Based on Jewish tradition, the universe was created on this day culminating on the sixth day, which is when Adam, the first man was created. This was the first day 'the kingdom of God' was established on the Earth as Adam was crowned King as a physical representation of the invisible King or Father himself. In line with Jewish traditions, the Kingship of God is also celebrated at this time with resounding trumpets that not only announce a new year but also the coming of His Kingdom on Earth in the past, present and future tense.

What we are seeing here, is that Eternity has fixed points of reference that exist both in the past and the future. The Apostle Paul describes a future event that happens at the end of the age which is preceded with the sound of a trumpet.

> Brothers and sisters, we do not want you to be uninformed about those who sleep in death, so that you do not grieve like the rest of mankind, who have no hope. For we believe that Jesus died and rose again, and so we believe that God will bring with Jesus those who have fallen asleep in him. According to the Lord's word, we tell you that we who are still alive, who are left until the coming of the Lord, will certainly not precede those who have fallen asleep. For the Lord himself will come down from heaven, with a loud

command, with the voice of the archangel and with the trumpet call of God, and the dead in Christ will rise first. After that, we who are still alive and are left will be caught up together with them in the clouds to meet the Lord in the air. And so we will be with the Lord forever.

1 Thessalonians 4:13-17

I declare to you, brothers and sisters, that flesh and blood cannot inherit the kingdom of God, nor does the perishable inherit the imperishable. Listen, I tell you a mystery: We will not all sleep, but we will all be changed—in a flash, in the twinkling of an eye, at the last trumpet. For the trumpet will sound, the dead will be raised imperishable, and we will be changed.

1 Corinthians 15:50-52

At some point in the future, after the blast of that trumpet, the dead in Christ are raised from the dead and the feast of trumpets will serve as a prelude to a glorious day. According to Jewish traditions, it is also said that this day marks the beginning of 10 'Days of Awe' which culminates with 'Yom Kippur' or the Day of Atonement. Where the scales of judgement are weighed in the Heavens and the determination of the immediate future.

The Day of Atonement

The tenth day of the seventh month is called the 'Day of Atonement'. The Jewish people call this Yom Kippur. Historically, on this day, the designated High Priest would provide sacrifice two out of three animals (one bull and two goats) and sprinkle their blood in the holiest place of the tabernacle Moses built after the exodus from Egypt. The High Priest would lay his hand on the head of the animals transferring the sins of his household, priesthood and the nation of Israel. One bull and one goat would then be slaughtered and the second goat would be led away from the city into the wilderness with a scarlet rope tied around its neck. This would signify the peoples' sin leaving the city and thus becoming a 'scapegoat'. The High Priest would then take the blood of the animals, enter the Most Holy Place and sprinkle the blood on the Mercy Seat to bring 'atonement' for the sins of the nation for a whole year.

The tabernacle had three different compartments with varying objects and equipment. The first compartment was called the 'Outer Court', the second the 'Holy Place' and the third contained the most significant object called the 'Ark of the Covenant'. This compartment was separated by a thick curtain and was called the 'Holy of Holies' or 'Most Holy Place'. It was the place where God lived or "the Holiest place of all". It was said that God's presence was so strong that if the correct protocol wasn't followed, people would actually die. Of all the priesthood that operated in the tabernacle, only the High Priest could perform the Atonement ceremony once a year which would bring the nation to a place of at-one-ment with God.

This prophetic drama would continue for years and serve as a precursor until the coming of Jesus. Once sentenced to death, Jesus carried his cross through the streets of Jerusalem and was crucified OUTSIDE of the city. The following passage in the book of Hebrews describes what happened when Jesus ascended after His resurrection.

> But when Christ came as high priest of the good things that
> are now already here,[a] he went through the greater and

more perfect tabernacle that is not made with human hands, that is to say, is not a part of this creation. He did not enter by means of the blood of goats and calves; but he entered the Most Holy Place once for all by his own blood, thus obtaining[b] eternal redemption. The blood of goats and bulls and the ashes of a heifer sprinkled on those who are ceremonially unclean sanctify them so that they are outwardly clean. How much more, then, will the blood of Christ, who through the eternal Spirit offered himself unblemished to God, cleanse our consciences from acts that lead to death,[c] so that we may serve the living God!

For Christ did not enter a sanctuary made with human hands that was only a copy of the true one; he entered heaven itself, now to appear for us in God's presence. Nor did he enter heaven to offer himself again and again, the way the high priest enters the Most Holy Place every year with blood that is not his own. Otherwise Christ would have had to suffer many times since the creation of the world. But he has appeared once for all at the culmination of the ages to do away with sin by the sacrifice of himself. Just as people are destined to die once, and after that to face judgment, so Christ was sacrificed once to take away the sins of many; and he will appear a second time, not to bear sin, but to bring salvation to those who are waiting for him.
Hebrews 9:11-14, 24-28

What the High Priests were doing for many years, was speaking to a future time when Jesus would bring us all into at-one-ment with Father once and for all. As the innocent One had to pay a price for the guilty as sin was being judged. This feast also points to the future as the Bible reveals that every man, women and nation will be judged at some point in the future. There is an appointed day of reckoning coming, Yom Kippur signifies this. However, I am so thankful that Father made a way for sin to be dealt with through His Son, Jesus.

Tabernacles

The Feast of Tabernacles or Succoth is Jewish terminology for "the last of the Feasts". Again, this feast, like Passover speaks to Israel's history as well as the future. When the nation was making its transition in the wilderness from slavery into the land of promise, they lived in temporary accommodations of tents or booths. They would move from place to place living this way until arriving in Israel where permanent places of abode were eventually built (i.e. houses).

It is a feast that celebrates Father's protection as well as His provision for His people during that time. It also celebrates His decision to live amongst His people in the Tent of Meeting or what is commonly known as the Tabernacle of Moses. In ancient Israel, their descendants were charged annually to take the journey to Jerusalem and make temporary booths/huts and share a brief experience of what their ancestors endured during their 40-year sojourn from Egypt.

It also was a harvest celebration, when the final harvest or ingathering took place. Only at the end of the agricultural year could the complete harvest be celebrated. This Feast became so popular it became known as 'THE FEAST'. Being the last of the feasts it also communicates the future in a unique way. Primarily, through its agricultural settings but according to the passage below, the Apostle

Paul gives additional insight and describes the coming of the Holy Spirit as a deposit being paid down.

> 'And you also were included in Christ when you heard the message of truth, the gospel of your salvation. When you believed, you were marked in him with a seal, the promised Holy Spirit, who is a deposit guaranteeing our inheritance until the redemption of those who are God's possession—to the praise of his glory.'
> **Ephesians 1:13-14**

A deposit is normally paid with the promise of full payment at a later date. As glorious as the coming of the Holy Spirit was, something more glorious is on its way as Father is bringing His church into Fullness, the FULL inheritance that Jesus paid for. The celebrations relating to the harvest could only be fully completed when the FULLNESS of the harvest came in during this feast. In other words, the Church celebrates Pentecost but should be looking for something far greater as Tabernacles is THE feast relating to the days, we live in. The Bible describes harvesting taking place in the last days that separate the wheat from the tares

There comes a time at the end of this age when the systems of this world will finally be overcome. All of Christ's enemies will be placed under His feet and the dawning of a new age begins. The prophetic writings of Zechariah confirm this when describing the 'Day of the Lord'. He envisions a time in the future when the Lord himself arrives to fight the nations that will come to invade and destroy Jerusalem. The Lord Jesus will arrive on the Mount of Olives and split the mountain in two, proceeding to rescue Jerusalem from its enemies; hence beginning His reign over ALL the nations.

'The Lord will be king over the whole earth. On that day
there will be one Lord, and his name the only name.'
Zechariah 14:8

Further on in that chapter, Zechariah describes the compulsory
worship that will occur at that point in the future which provides
insight into the rule of King Jesus over the nations.

'Then the survivors from all the nations that have attacked
Jerusalem will go up year after year to worship the King, the
Lord Almighty, and to celebrate the Festival of Tabernacles.'
Zechariah 14:16a

This feast is celebrated not only in this age but in the age to come.
This point is made clear in the book of Revelation where the Apostle
John writes;

'And I heard a great voice out of heaven saying, Behold, the
tabernacle of God is with men, and he will dwell with them,
and they shall be his people, and God himself shall be with
them, and be their God And God shall wipe away all tears
from their eyes; and there shall be no more death, neither
sorrow, nor crying, neither shall there be any more pain: for
the former things are passed away.'
Revelation 21:3-4 King James Version

This feast also points to this incredible event, witnessed by the
Apostle John during the visions of the future he received while in
exile on the Isle of Patmos. The tabernacle of God comes out of
Heaven and descends to the New Earth and remains a permanent
fixture for the rest of Eternity. Our current distress on the Earth will

be a thing of the past with no more death or sufferings. These realities do have a time limit as the age to come is on its way.

Synchronization

Daniel was a teenager when he and others were sent to Babylon as captives after Jerusalem had fallen to King Nebuchadnezzar in 605 BC. Being a noble, he was sent to work in the Royal Courts of Babylon as an advisor/administrator serving in a governmental capacity with both the Babylonian and Persian empires. He was renowned for his wisdom and excellence having authored the Book of Daniel, arguably the most prophetic book of the Bible. In this book, Daniel receives insight into the future, as he accurately describes emerging world powers/kingdoms and the coming eternal kingdom of God through Jesus. In the ninth chapter of his book, Daniel has a unique visitation from the Angel Gabriel, a messenger or herald type of Angel. This angel had visited him earlier with a profound interpretation of a vision he received outlining the rise of future world empires (Persian/Medes and the rise of the Greek empire via Alexander the Great).

The background for this visitation was when Daniel prayed over a prophetic word given by a prophet called Jeremiah who warned the leaders of the Kingdom of Judah for over 25 years that the Babylonians were coming. He prophesied that they would invade Jerusalem due to generations of moral decay in the nation and the city would be taken with its people held captive to Babylonia. Jeremiah prophesied and wrote that this state of affairs would last 70 years. Upon reading Jeremiah's writings Daniel calculated that this seventy-year period was coming to an end and immediately entered a time of fasting and prayer. This moment of prayer activated and synchronized Heaven and Earth, setting into motion a chain of events that would lead to Jerusalem's restoration. While Daniel is confessing his own sins and the sins of his people, Gabriel suddenly appears and gives him insight into Jerusalem's future.

> While I was still in prayer, Gabriel, the man I had seen in the earlier vision, came to me in swift flight about the time of the evening sacrifice. He instructed me and said to me, "Daniel, I have now come to give you insight and understanding. As soon as you began to pray, a word went out, which I have come to tell you, for you are highly esteemed. Therefore, consider the word and understand the vision:

> "Seventy 'sevens'[c] are decreed for your people and your holy city to finish[d] transgression, to put an end to sin, to atone for wickedness, to bring in everlasting righteousness, to seal up vision and prophecy and to anoint the Most Holy Place.[e]

> "Know and understand this: From the time the word goes out to restore and rebuild Jerusalem until the Anointed One,[f] the ruler, comes, there will be seven 'sevens,' and sixty-two 'sevens.' It will be rebuilt with streets and a trench, but in times of trouble. After the sixty-two 'sevens,' the Anointed One will be put to death and will have nothing.[g] The people of the ruler who will come will destroy the city and the sanctuary. The end will come like a flood: War will continue until the end, and desolations have been decreed.
> Daniel 9:21-25

Gabriel releases an insight into Jerusalem's future with a timescale of 'seventy weeks' which is prophetic terminology for exactly 70, seven-year periods. At the time, Jerusalem was desolate but Gabriel reveals that the city would be restored and rebuilt. Once that decree was established, the timescale would be set into motion and after 69, seven-year periods, the Messiah would not only appear but be put to death. A brief history lesson will reveal how accurate this prophetic decree was.

Artaxerxes, the Persian ruler of Babylon made a decree to restore and rebuild Jerusalem in the month of Nissan (March/April) in 444 B.C thus sending Nehemiah who was originally a cupbearer as a Governor to Jerusalem, to complete the task. The 69 seven-year periods would then start from that date. Calculations say that 69 seven-year periods equate to 483 years. Exactly 483 years after this decree, Jesus is entering Jerusalem on a donkey with verbal acclamations and one week later He is crucified. The prophetic information also revealed that soon after the Lord's crucifixion, the city and the temple would be destroyed by 'the people of the ruler'. According to historians, Titus a Roman General and his armies came and destroyed the temple and the city in 70 AD.

There's one more 'week' or period of seven years still earmarked for Jerusalem that will happen in the future, where a ruler will arise to rule in two periods of three and a half years. Most bible scholars attribute this to be the coming Anti-Christ and his time of domination in the earth.

The Entrance of the Son.

After the return of the Exiles from Babylon and into the time of Caesar Augustus, Judea is now under Roman subjugation. Suddenly the heavens are stirred as an appointed time which was birthed and purposed in Eternity finally reaches 'time'. This event would shake and change the world forever, the entrance of the Son. The Apostle John describes it this way,

> In the beginning was the Word, and the Word was with God, and the Word was God. He was with God in the beginning. Through him all things were made; without him nothing was made that has been made. In him was life, and that life was the light of all mankind.
>
> The Word became flesh and made his dwelling among us. We have seen his glory, the glory of the one and only Son, who came from the Father, full of grace and truth.'
> **John 1:1-4 & 14**

Fifteen months prior to the Lord's birth, angelic and prophetic activity is stirred after 400 years of silence. According to the Gospel of Luke, the Angel Gabriel shows up again centuries after his interactions with Daniel and appears in the Temple in Jerusalem to an old priest called Zechariah (the father of John the Baptist). The angel says he is going to have a son and to call his name John. Gabriel gives Zechariah insight into the future informing him that John would indeed be a forerunner, preparing the way for the promised Messiah. Zechariah was old and his wife Elizabeth was way past the age for childbearing. Once his duties were completed in the temple, Zechariah returned home to the hill country of Judea and his wife conceived. Six months after this, Gabriel is despatched to meet and send a message to a young lady in Galilee. The Gospel of Luke records this remarkable event.

> In the sixth month of Elizabeth's pregnancy, God sent the angel Gabriel to Nazareth, a town in Galilee, to a virgin pledged to be married to a man named Joseph, a descendant

THE FUTURENOW

of David. The virgin's name was Mary. The angel went to her and said, "Greetings, you who are highly favoured! The Lord is with you."

Mary was greatly troubled at his words and wondered what kind of greeting this might be. But the angel said to her, "Do not be afraid, Mary; you have found favour with God. You will conceive and give birth to a son, and you are to call him Jesus. He will be great and will be called the Son of the Most High. The Lord God will give him the throne of his father David, and he will reign over Jacob's descendants forever; his kingdom will never end."

How will this be," Mary asked the angel, "since I am a virgin?"

The angel answered, "The Holy Spirit will come on you, and the power of the Most High will overshadow you. So the holy one to be born will be called[b] the Son of God. Even Elizabeth your relative is going to have a child in her old age, and she who was said to be unable to conceive is in her sixth month. For no word from God will ever fail."

"I am the Lord's servant," Mary answered. "May your word to me be fulfilled." Then the angel left her.
St Luke 1:26-38

Again, the prophetic discourse from Gabriel reveals the future of Mary's Son and the impact He will have on the nations and ultimately the world. Mary and Elizabeth were cousins, so after the visitation from Gabriel, Mary decides to visit Elizabeth. Upon meeting her, the baby in Elizabeth's womb jumps and both of them

28

begin to prophesy under the influence of the Holy Spirit. Elizabeth prophetically declares the following not knowing that the angel Gabriel had visited Mary and what he had told her.

'When Elizabeth heard Mary's greeting, the baby leaped in her womb, and Elizabeth was filled with the Holy Spirit. 42In a loud voice she exclaimed: "Blessed are you among women, and blessed is the child you will bear! 43But why am I so favored, that the mother of my Lord should come to me? 44As soon as the sound of your greeting reached my ears, the baby in my womb leaped for joy. 45Blessed is she who has believed that the Lord would fulfill his promises to her!"

And Mary said:
"My soul glorifies the Lord
and my spirit rejoices in God my Savior,
for he has been mindful
of the humble state of his servant.
From now on all generations will call me blessed,
for the Mighty One has done great things for me—
holy is his name.
His mercy extends to those who fear him,
from generation to generation.
He has performed mighty deeds with his arm;
he has scattered those who are proud in their inmost thoughts.
He has brought down rulers from their thrones
but has lifted up the humble.
He has filled the hungry with good things
but has sent the rich away empty.
He has helped his servant Israel,
remembering to be merciful

to Abraham and his descendants forever,
just as he promised our ancestors."
Luke 1:41-55

Soon thereafter John was born and the prophetic activity continues.
When asked to name him, Elizabeth insists the boy's name is to be
called John not observing the family tradition. When relatives
approached her husband Zechariah, who since the visitation from
Gabriel was struck dumb due to his unbelief. He asked for a writing
tablet and wrote 'His name is John'. His tongue was set free and he
began praising God and prophesied the following.

His father Zechariah was filled with the Holy Spirit and
prophesied:
"Praise be to the Lord, the God of Israel,
because he has come to his people and redeemed them.
He has raised up a horn[c] of salvation for us
in the house of his servant David
(as he said through his holy prophets of long ago),
salvation from our enemies
and from the hand of all who hate us—
to show mercy to our ancestors
and to remember his holy covenant,
the oath he swore to our father Abraham:
to rescue us from the hand of our enemies,
and to enable us to serve him without fear
in holiness and righteousness before him all our days.
And you, my child, will be called a prophet of the Most High;
for you will go on before the Lord to prepare the way for him,
to give his people the knowledge of salvation
through the forgiveness of their sins,
because of the tender mercy of our God,

by which the rising sun will come to us from heaven
to shine on those living in darkness
and in the shadow of death,
to guide our feet into the path of peace."
Luke 1:61-79

When Jesus is born, Heaven and Earth synchronise for a moment, as more angelic and prophetic activity was released.

And there were shepherds living out in the fields nearby, keeping watch over their flocks at night. An angel of the Lord appeared to them, and the glory of the Lord shone around them, and they were terrified. But the angel said to them, "Do not be afraid. I bring you good news that will cause great joy for all the people. Today in the town of David a Savior has been born to you; he is the Messiah, the Lord. This will be a sign to you: You will find a baby wrapped in cloths and lying in a manger."

Suddenly a great company of the heavenly host appeared with the angel, praising God and saying,

"Glory to God in the highest heaven,
and on earth peace to those on whom his favor rests."

When the angels had left them and gone into heaven, the shepherds said to one another, "Let's go to Bethlehem and see this thing that has happened, which the Lord has told us about." So they hurried off and found Mary and Joseph, and the baby, who was lying in the manger. When they had seen him, they spread the word concerning what had been told them about this child, and all who heard it were amazed at

what the shepherds said to them. But Mary treasured up all these things and pondered them in her heart. The shepherds returned, glorifying and praising God for all the things they had heard and seen, which were just as they had been told.
Luke 2:8-20

Now there was a man in Jerusalem called Simeon, who was righteous and devout. He was waiting for the consolation of Israel, and the Holy Spirit was on him. It had been revealed to him by the Holy Spirit that he would not die before he had seen the Lord's Messiah. Moved by the Spirit, he went into the temple courts. When the parents brought in the child Jesus to do for him what the custom of the Law required, Simeon took him in his arms and praised God, saying:

"Sovereign Lord, as you have promised,
you may now dismiss[d] your servant in peace.
For my eyes have seen your salvation,
which you have prepared in the sight of all nations:
light for revelation to the Gentiles,
and the glory of your people Israel."
Luke 2:25-32

As a side note, the main reason for highlighting these series of events is for you to see the prophetic information released and how it's tense is generally 'present-future'. At that time in Israel's history, only a few people were aware of what the Lord was up to during that particular season. This should serve as an encouragement for prophetic people as on many occasions, insight into the present and the future is often given to the few and not the mainstream. If you are carrying a dream or an aspect of the future, you cannot be a follower of the mainstream and do not allow the 'tyranny' of the present' to abort what has been placed in you.

Eternal Fixed Points

The entrance of the Son was planned and purposed in Eternity. Jesus's birth released a line of demarcation or what I call fixed points which exists in both Eternity and Time. The way time is measured presently is by using this line of demarcation. Using the Gregorian calendar, the years before and after Jesus's birth is designated as B.C. or before Christ and A.D. (Anno Domini which translates to 'the year of our Lord') respectively. For example, at the time of writing this book, we are in the year 2019 A.D., which means that 2019 years have passed since Jesus was born.

As previously explained, the Jewish feasts point to these 'fixed points' in Eternity where they foreshadowed key moments of huge significance in Jesus's life and mission. Mainly, His birth, death, resurrection and ascension. He suffered for our sins, sicknesses, curses and paid the price to redeem us all. He rose from the grave defeating death making a mockery of the enemy and now lives forevermore. He ascended into the Heavens, and as a High Priest presented His life's blood on the mercy seat bringing us all 'at-one-ment' with the Father. The significance of this should never be underestimated, for as a result, through Jesus every obstacle to an empowering, loving relationship with the Father has now been removed PERMANENTLY. We have all now been made SONS and nothing will ever change that.

Although in time this event took place approx. two thousand years ago, in the realm of Eternity, Jesus's sacrifice is as fresh as the day it happened. It is a 'fixed point' that changed the world forever.

Everything in Heaven is 'Now' and moves from moment to moment depending on the seasons there. This is the reason that if anyone, anywhere at any time calls on His name whether in the gutter or the palace, it activates the realities of being 'at-one-ment' and faith brings that reality into manifestation.

Faith accesses these Eternal 'fixed points' and brings the reality of that Heavenly transaction out of the realm of the supernatural into the natural. This is what happened to me on 22nd February 1987 at a church in Kilburn, North West London. After hearing the preaching of the Gospel, prayed and accepted the Lordship of Jesus into my life. Not quite understanding the theology or why but knowing that at that moment this was my time. There was no lightning or thunder but I knew something had changed inside of me as the Holy Spirit brought to me right there, the fullness of what Jesus died and paid for.

I was a teenager at the time and was experimenting with drugs, girls and on the cusp of street life. However, the 'High' I felt that night, nothing on Earth can compare to it and my journey with the Father began and continues to this day. These fixed points reveal what is termed the 'finished works of Christ' and is the Source of all supernatural activity in the church. In other words, your salvation, healing, miracle and deliverance has been 'paid for' and is always accessible by faith at any time.

Eternity Within

We understand that Eternity is the original time zone and that time as we know it was created and operates concurrently with it. Referring to Diagram 2, it shows that time is housed within Eternity.

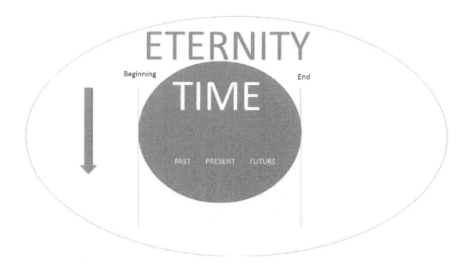

Here we see that the 'past, present and future is housed within Eternity. To further cement this point the Apostle John received visions and insight into the future while in exile on the Isle of Patmos. His writings are known as the book of 'Revelation' and is another profound prophetic book in the Bible.

The book of Revelation is often misunderstood because many of us miss an important truth of 'WHO' the book is about in the first place. Many Christian commentators are so focused on a one-world government, led by a charismatic leader (the Anti-Christ) and the supposed end of the world scenario. Rather than the ultimate victory over evil, the coming of the rule of Christ and the dawn of a new age. This has given us a narrative of the future that has made the church unable to discern the times in which we live in and play our part in bringing transformation to our society. I believe that our current eschatology needs to be revisited with fresh eyes. I will not be ending this chapter with an expose' on the book of Revelation but rather remind you of 'WHO' it is about and to do that I will let John speak for himself by highlighting these scriptures:

The Revelation of Jesus Christ, which God gave unto him, to shew unto his servants things which must shortly come to pass; and he sent and signified it by his angel unto his servant John:

Who bare record of the word of God, and of the testimony of Jesus Christ, and of all things that he saw.

Blessed is he that readeth, and they that hear the words of this prophecy, and keep those things which are written therein: for the time is at hand.
Revelation 1:1-3

The true title of this book according to the Apostle is 'the Revelation of Jesus Christ'. John was one of the Lord's disciples and travelled with Him for over three years. He had first- hand knowledge of Jesus' ministry, death and resurrection along with direct conversations with the Lord before His death and after He had risen. It would be fair to say that prior to his exile on Patmos, John had and was working with a revelation on who Jesus is.

Since the basic way of defining the word revelation would be the 'uncovering of that which is hidden' so, conceivably John begins to see Jesus 'uncovered' in a new way which creates a vision of how the future appears. His experience on the Isle of Patmos, discloses Jesus in a way he had never seen before and also reveals the Kingship of Jesus and its impact on Israel, the Gentiles, the Church and the world system in the future. This prophetic book is so vivid and uses imagery to convey coded messages regarding the future. It also gives insight into the dynamics of Heaven and how it affects the earth. John describes a culmination of 'appointed times and seasons' for all four of the above and the coming of Jesus's rule on the Earth. In other words, there are three major phases of transition coming to our world and political system especially in the West. The transition from firstly democracy to totalitarian rule for a short period, and then ultimately a transition into a theocracy. In the midst of these experiences, John writes something quite profound:

> After this I looked, and there before me was a door standing open in heaven. And the voice I had first heard speaking to me like a trumpet said, "Come up here, and I will show you what must take place after this."
> **Revalation 4:1**

Notice, he heard the instruction to 'COME UP HERE'. Where is 'here'? John explains in the next verses when he is taken up into the Highest Vantage Point there is; the Throne Room in Heaven where the original time zone governs. It was in this place, that John sees events and days that have not come 'down' to the Earth yet. This indicates that this realm called Eternity houses your future, my future and the future of the whole world.

> To every thing there is a season, and a time to every purpose under the heaven:
>
> A time to be born, and a time to die; a time to plant, and a time to pluck up that which is planted;
>
> A time to kill, and a time to heal; a time to break down, and a time to build up;
>
> A time to weep, and a time to laugh; a time to mourn, and a time to dance;

A time to cast away stones, and a time to gather stones together; a time to embrace, and a time to refrain from embracing;

A time to get, and a time to lose; a time to keep, and a time to cast away;

A time to rend, and a time to sew; a time to keep silence, and a time to speak;

A time to love, and a time to hate; a time of war, and a time of peace.

What profit hath he that worketh in that wherein he laboureth?

I have seen the travail, which God hath given to the sons of men to be exercised in it.

He hath made every thing beautiful in his time: also he hath set the world in their heart, so that no man can find out the work that God maketh from the beginning to the end.
Ecclesiastes 3:1-11

This scripture discusses the cycles and the seasons in life but an excerpt in Verse eleven reveals a powerful truth that forms the basis of this particular chapter. It says that 'He (God) has set the 'world' in their heart'. Further research and study conveys a startling revelation, the word 'world' here is translated from Hebrew to mean something other than the world or its systems.

The word here is 'olam' and it is one of two Hebrew words to describe time. The first is 'Eth' this describes time in a general sense and can include appointed times and season. 'Olam' however is translated as indefinite time or Eternity. The word 'heart' comes from the Hebrew word 'Leb' which means the centre, middle or core of anything. In this instance, the inner person with a focus on the psychological aspects of the mind and heart.

As previously indicated, the realm of Eternity governs Heaven and the invisible world but according to this verse, it has also been placed in the heart of man. That is the reason, why you instinctively know things because Eternity has also been placed within you. This also means that an aspect of our future has been placed WITHIN us. According to the book of Proverbs, we may well need 'a man or woman of understanding' to draw it out.

Conclusively, your personality, character, gifting mixes have all been predetermined, you are living here ON and FOR purpose. You, my friend, have been brought to the Kingdom for such a time as this and your best days are in front of you not behind.

Chapter Three

The Language of Faith

In this chapter, we will be taking a closer look at a vital component for a FutureNow Lifestyle. This component is known as 'Faith'. To accomplish this, we must direct our attention to Abraham and how faith impacted his life, enabling him to journey into the future.

Abraham began life as Abram and lived in the city of Ur (Iraq). He was married to Sarai and was a successful businessman who traded gold, silver, cattle and goats. His life was going well with one exception; he and his wife are childless. However, at the age of 75, the future visits him in the form of a prophetic word that changes his life forever.

> "Now the Lord had said unto Abram, Get thee out of thy country, and from thy kindred, and from thy father's house, unto a land that I will shew thee:
>
> And I will make of thee a great nation, and I will bless thee, and make thy name great; and thou shalt be a blessing:
>
> And I will bless them that bless thee, and curse him that curseth thee: and in thee shall all families of the earth be blessed.

So Abram departed, as the Lord had spoken unto him; and
Lot went with him: and Abram was seventy and five years
old when he departed out of Haran.
Genesis 12:1-4

After leaving the city of Haran, Abram arrives in the land of Canaan
and the Lord speaks to him again.

And the Lord appeared unto Abram, and said, Unto thy seed
will I give this land: and there builded he an altar unto the
Lord, who appeared unto him.
Genesis 12:7

He has now reached the land promised him. As a businessman,
Abram presumably starts trading and mixes with the local
inhabitants experiencing the smell, the culture and seeing the
resources with his own eyes. During this time Abram is given a
promise that one day his descendants will own the land he is
currently living in. The future revealed to Abram is no longer just
contained in words, it is now tangible becoming more possible. The
prophetic word given begins to open Abram up to new possibilities
and begin the process of the future becoming a reality in his life.

After spending some time in Egypt, he returns the land of Canaan
and again is living and trading in the land. When his nephew, Lot
leaves due to a business conflict, Abram receives the following
promise as the future speaks again and changes his viewpoint.

And the Lord said unto Abram, after that Lot was separated
from him, Lift up now thine eyes, and look from the place
where thou art northward, and southward, and eastward,
and westward:

For all the land which thou seest, to thee will I give it, and to thy seed for ever.

And I will make thy seed as the dust of the earth: so that if a man can number the dust of the earth, then shall thy seed also be numbered.

Arise, walk through the land in the length of it and in the breadth of it; for I will give it unto thee.
Genesis 13:14-17

In other words, Abram 'take a panoramic view' of what I have promised. Break out of the limitations of the present and the 'patch' of land that you are trading in. Don't allow the present to limit your imaginations. Lift up your eyes and LOOK FURTHER. Your descendants will be innumerable and inhabit the land as far as your eyes can see. In fact Abram, now 'walk' through the length and breadth of the land that your descendants will one day possess and experience the Future, NOW.

Seeing

To begin speaking the language of faith your 'seeing' must first change.

Now faith is the substance of things hoped for, the evidence of things not seen.

For by it the elders obtained a good report.

Through faith we understand that the worlds were framed by the word of God, so that things which are seen were not made of things which do appear.
Hebrews 11:1-3

The verse above describes what faith is. It is the substance of things hoped for. This substance is so powerful that it was used to frame the worlds as we know them. It is a substance from the realm Eternal. Faith caused what the Lord imagined to materialise in the physical realm when He spoke the worlds into being during creation. Faith is the substance or a firm foundation of the things 'hoped for' and the proof/evidence that those thing's actually exist. Faith is more than confessions, when fully utilized it will become a lifestyle where the possibilities of what is 'hoped for' becomes a reality. Faith is the substance or a firm foundation. Due to the limitations of the English language, there is a genuine misunderstanding of what 'hope' really means in the biblical sense. Hope in the above scripture reading can be categorized as things that we earnestly expect. So in a sense, faith is the substance of things earnestly expected sometime in the future. This could be a vision, dream or goal but hope earnestly expects it to happen.

I grew up in North West London where the bus services were substandard. We even had what we called a 'Ghost Bus' because at the time it was so rarely seen. We would wait for the #112 at your own peril, as that service was something else. Now when waiting for the bus after school, I knew the bus was coming but didn't know when it would arrive. Many times I gave up and just walked home, relinquishing all hope that a bus is coming; only to see two or three buses arriving in a row while walking home. The point I am making is that, standing at the bus stop on most occasions I earnestly expected one to come. I would 'look' up the road to 'see' whether one was coming or not. Based on the information given to me by the timetable, I would stand there waiting, 'knowing' eventually a bus would come. Living in faith is similar, as the things 'hoped for' is often the future revealed. Faith presumes that the future revealed is a reality and in so doing modifies our thinking and behaviour accordingly. The Apostle Paul says it this way:

'For we walk by faith, not by sight'
2 Corinthians 5:7

He is not talking about walking as in walking up the road. The word walk here is indicative of a lifestyle that is governed by faith and not on what one can see. We will now again take a look at Abram's life and see how faith played an integral part in his destiny. Abram has now lived in Canaan for up to 10 years. His journey of faith is wavering as both he and his wife are getting older. At this moment the Lord initiates a process that solidifies Abram's faith forever:

After these things the word of the Lord came unto Abram in a vision, saying, Fear not, Abram: I am thy shield, and thy exceeding great reward.

And Abram said, Lord God, what wilt thou give me, seeing I go childless, and the steward of my house is this Eliezer of Damascus?

And Abram said, Behold, to me thou hast given no seed: and, lo, one born in my house is mine heir.

And, behold, the word of the Lord came unto him, saying, This shall not be thine heir; but he that shall come forth out of thine own bowels shall be thine heir.

And he brought him forth abroad, and said, Look now toward heaven, and tell the stars, if thou be able to number them: and he said unto him, So shall thy seed be.

And he believed in the Lord; and he counted it to him for righteousness.

And he said unto him, I am the Lord that brought thee out of Ur of the Chaldees, to give thee this land to inherit it.
Genesis 15:1-7

All Abram could 'see' at this time in his life is that he and Sarai were still barren after all these years. The facts are plain to see, so in the above passage his 'language' reflects as much. In order to change this, the Lord brought Abram out of his 'tent' to look at the stars in the night sky. Abram was focusing on what was happening within his tent and the limitations of his circumstances. By coming out of the tent and gazing at the stars, he opened his mind/imaginations to fresh possibilities. The Lord asked him to number the stars if he could, because that is how numerous Abram's descendants would be. Abram was again challenged to 'see' his Future Now. In doing so, Abram broke every limitation in his life and something changed internally as the passage says he now believed. He believed that the future revealed was true and that his descendants would be innumerable and inherit the land as promised. Abram's language begins to change after this encounter.

And he said, Lord God, whereby shall I know that I shall inherit it?

And he said unto him, Take me an heifer of three years old, and a she goat of three years old, and a ram of three years old, and a turtledove, and a young pigeon.

And he took unto him all these, and divided them in the midst, and laid each piece one against another: but the birds divided he not.
Genesis 15:8-10

Abram's new level of faith prompts a question that the Lord responds to. A blood covenant ceremony familiar to Abram and the culture of that time was started. This concept of blood covenants was established in the ancient world, where two parties would agree to come together and bind themselves to a covenant for mutual gain.

During this ceremony, animals would be sacrificed and split in two, the blood spilt would be in the midst of the two pieces. Once the ceremony is completed, both parties would walk between the animal pieces which would be a method of 'signing' the covenant. On this occasion, only one person 'signed' the covenant.

The closest thing we have in the western world are contracts, which are signed and sealed by signatures. The two parties would do everything in their power to accomplish the terms of the covenant with grave consequences if the covenant is broken.

When the sun had set and darkness had fallen, a smoking fire pot with a blazing torch appeared and passed between the pieces. On that day the Lord made a covenant with Abram and said, "To your descendants I give this land, from the Wadi[e] of Egypt to the great river, the Euphrates—the land of the Kenites, Kenizzites, Kadmonites, Hittites, Perizzites, Rephaites, Amorites, Canaanites, Girgashites and Jebusites."
Genesis 15:17-20

After this encounter, Abram never again wavered because He had a 'guarantee' from the One who created the universe. In this transaction, God not only became a covenant partner with him, but also the One who would use His considerable and unlimited abilities to honour His promise. Take a moment and absorb the reality of this and realise that it is not too dissimilar to what the Lord has done for us in our day. Father has invited all of us to a covenant relationship/partnership through His Son, Jesus Christ. The power of this covenant was revealed when Jesus rose from the dead and ascended into heaven. Which means He has the power to bring you into your promise, just like he did for Abram.

Looking at Abram's situation, his future seemed so farfetched, out of reach. This is normally a sign whether your dream is from the Lord or not. If you are able to make your future or dream happen with your own talents or abilities then it is not sourced from the Father. However, if even with your talents/abilities, you fall woefully short of what has been revealed, then, like Abram the impossible is made possible through the One who sourced the dream in the first place. Jesus did not only redeem us from our sins, He also redeemed our FUTURE. As with Abram, when your viewpoint changes, your 'language' also follows suit.

When faith operates in our hearts, it gives us access to the supernatural. It is the substance the future is made of. It governs time and we can see an example of it in this passage of scripture. His faith not only prompted the covenant-making ceremony, but also opened up a more detailed look into the future.

Abram 'sees' what is going to happen to him, his descendants and the inhabitants currently living in the land of promise. The future of the region and of his descendants is revealed spanning the next

400 years. Moses' and Joshua's (Abram's descendants) stories are told right there, hundreds of years before they were born and prior to the Exodus from Egypt.

> As the sun was setting, Abram fell into a deep sleep, and a thick and dreadful darkness came over him. Then the Lord said to him, "Know for certain that for four hundred years your descendants will be strangers in a country not their own and that they will be enslaved and mistreated there. But I will punish the nation they serve as slaves, and afterward they will come out with great possessions. You, however, will go to your ancestors in peace and be buried at a good old age. In the fourth generation your descendants will come back here, for the sin of the Amorites has not yet reached its full measure."
> **Genesis 15:12-16**

Kairos Time

Every prophetic word or promise comes with an inbuilt 'timespan' for it's fulfilment. The Greek word 'kairos' is used when describing this aspect of time. It means an 'appointed time or season'. Abram has reached 99 years of age and has entered into a kairos season in his life, the appointed time for Isaac's birth is rapidly approaching. It's at this moment, supernatural activity increases and Abram has a visitation from the Lord.

> And when Abram was ninety years old and nine, the Lord appeared to Abram, and said unto him, I am the Almighty God; walk before me, and be thou perfect.
>
> And I will make my covenant between me and thee, and will multiply thee exceedingly.

And Abram fell on his face: and God talked with him, saying,

As for me, behold, my covenant is with thee, and thou shalt be a father of many nations.

Neither shall thy name any more be called Abram, but thy name shall be Abraham; for a father of many nations have I made thee.

And I will make thee exceeding fruitful, and I will make nations of thee, and kings shall come out of thee.

And I will establish my covenant between me and thee and thy seed after thee in their generations for an everlasting covenant, to be a God unto thee, and to thy seed after thee.

And I will give unto thee, and to thy seed after thee, the land wherein thou art a stranger, all the land of Canaan, for an everlasting possession; and I will be their God.
Genesis 17:1-8

In this encounter, Father changes Abram's name to Abraham. The name Abram means 'Exalted Father' but the name Abraham means 'Father of many nations'. The language of faith is now being spoken, calling the revealed future into manifestation. The conversation continues as the Lord instructs a name change for Sarai too.

And God said unto Abraham, As for Sarai thy wife, thou shalt not call her name Sarai, but Sarah shall her name be.

And I will bless her, and give thee a son also of her: yea, I will bless her, and she shall be a mother of nations; kings of people shall be of her.
Genesis 17:15-16

Sarai means 'My princess' and in this case, Sarah means 'Mother of many nations'. From that moment on the couple was known by their new names. When anyone addressed them, they too were speaking directly into their future. It was in this atmosphere sourced by their 'new language' that the miracle of Isaac's birth occurs. Miracles need a corresponding environment for them to manifest and an atmosphere charged with faith is one of them. Summarising Abraham's faith and describing the 'language' the Father uses, the Apostle Paul writes the following:

(As it is written, I have made thee a father of many nations,) before him whom he believed, even God, who quickeneth the dead, and calleth those things which be not as though they were.'
Romans 4:17

Father inhabits Eternity where the future is seen and known. This is why He speaks about the future even though there are no signs of it in the present. In this case, by calling Abram 'the father of many nations' the Lord was in effect calling the future into existence. When he changed Abrams' name, He was enlisting Abram's partnership to assist Him in doing so within chronological time. That call for partnership is what this whole chapter is about; understanding that the 'language of faith' is to a degree the language of the Future 'Now'. Faith is designed to 'connect' with the future revealed in Eternity and creates it here in this present slip of time. This is what I love about the Father, that no matter how dark things get, He has the capability to create new possibilities and timelines in accordance with His Eternal purposes. Later that year, Abraham experiences an unusual visitation, the Lord God in human form comes and visits his home. Genesis Chapter 18 captures this moment:

> And the Lord appeared unto him in the plains of Mamre: and he sat in the tent door in the heat of the day;
>
> And he lift up his eyes and looked, and, lo, three men stood by him: and when he saw them, he ran to meet them from the tent door, and bowed himself toward the ground,
>
> And said, My Lord, if now I have found favour in thy sight, pass not away, I pray thee, from thy servant:
>
> Let a little water, I pray you, be fetched, and wash your feet, and rest yourselves under the tree:
>
> And I will fetch a morsel of bread, and comfort ye your hearts; after that ye shall pass on: for therefore are ye come to your servant. And they said, So do, as thou hast said.
>
> And Abraham hastened into the tent unto Sarah, and said, Make ready quickly three measures of fine meal, knead it, and make cakes upon the hearth.
>
> And Abraham ran unto the herd, and fetcht a calf tender and good, and gave it unto a young man; and he hasted to dress it.
>
> And he took butter, and milk, and the calf which he had dressed, and set it before them; and he stood by them under the tree, and they did eat.

And they said unto him, Where is Sarah thy wife? And he said, Behold, in the tent.

And he said, I will certainly return unto thee according to the time of life; and, lo, Sarah thy wife shall have a son. And Sarah heard it in the tent door, which was behind him.

Now Abraham and Sarah were old and well stricken in age; and it ceased to be with Sarah after the manner of women.

Therefore Sarah laughed within herself, saying, After I am waxed old shall I have pleasure, my lord being old also?

And the Lord said unto Abraham, Wherefore did Sarah laugh, saying, Shall I of a surety bear a child, which am old?

Is any thing too hard for the Lord? At the time appointed I will return unto thee, according to the time of life, and Sarah shall have a son.
Genesis 18:1-14

There are so many truths in this passage, but for the sake of brevity, I will keep to the following points. As stated previously, Abraham had entered a Kairos season and while sitting outside his tent three men suddenly appear. He instantly recognises WHO had come to visit him, invites the men to refresh themselves and have a meal. It was while receiving Abraham's hospitality that the Lord informs him that his son Isaac is about to be born. The language of faith has now created an environment for the miracle to occur. Sarah was post-menopausal, her childbearing days were over and her womb was barren. However, when an atmosphere is charged with faith, the miraculous presents itself. In exactly the timespan given by the

Lord, Sarah conceives and the 'impossible' is cradled in her arms as Isaac is born.

> And the Lord visited Sarah as he had said, and the Lord did unto Sarah as he had spoken.
>
> For Sarah conceived, and bare Abraham a son in his old age, at the set time of which God had spoken to him.
>
> And Abraham called the name of his son that was born unto him, whom Sarah bare to him, Isaac.
>
> And Abraham circumcised his son Isaac being eight days old, as God had commanded him. 5And Abraham was an hundred years old, when his son Isaac was born unto him.
>
> And Sarah said, God hath made me to laugh, so that all that hear will laugh with me.
>
> And she said, Who would have said unto Abraham, that Sarah should have given children suck? for I have born him a son in his old age.
>
> **Genesis 21:1-7**

When you study Abraham's faith journey, you'll realise that he too had 'bumps in the road' and human frailties. Despite all of this, Father was true to His Word and now invites you to walk a fresh faith adventure with Him. A call is going out to find those who are willing to 'create' future timelines sourced in eternity for the times we currently live in. A new language needs to be spoken that corresponds with the future, the language called faith.

Chapter Four

The Future Speaks

Then the word of the Lord came unto me, saying,
Before I formed thee in the belly I knew thee; and before
thou camest forth out of the womb I sanctified thee, and I
ordained thee a prophet unto the nations.
Jeremiah 1:4-5

An excerpt of Jeremiah's call to the prophetic office reveals something that was true for him then and true for us today; you and I were 'known' and a purpose was assigned to us BEFORE we were conceived. In Jeremiah's case, the call to be a prophet in his times was what he was born for. The following diagram shows us where Jeremiah's purpose and ours are formed:

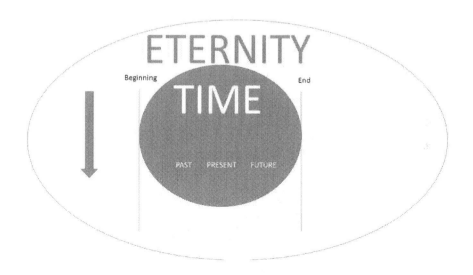

Your LIFE DREAM

I believe that a major part of the adventure called 'life' is about discovering what we were BORN FOR. It involves discovering who WE REALLY ARE and the purpose designed and allocated for us in Eternity. As discussed in Chapter two of this book, Father has set Eternity deep within our hearts. In other words, OUR PURPOSE and FUTURE lives within us. This, in most cases, manifest in what I call a 'Life Dream'. I am not talking about a crazy dream you may have after eating a dodgy pizza the night before. I am talking about dreaming with your eyes open: Things in life that you are inexplicably drawn to a deep desire that just won't go away, even when facing adverse circumstances and situations. I'm speaking of certain assignments that you might complete, if not for financial constraints and responsibilities or a thought or mental picture of the future that remains regardless of the challenges faced in your childhood. It could be a hope that keeps rising despite the numerous times life has knocked you down. I'm writing about THE dream that contains a coded future designed to change the world for the better; YOUR LIFE DREAM. Could it be that your LIFE DREAM is what this world is waiting for? Could your LIFE DREAM contain solutions that right now there's no answer for? Prophetically, I am declaring that your life dream is your FUTURE speaking to you. So many of us are chasing prophetic voices regarding aspects of our future, not recognising that our future resides to a degree within us and actually speaks. When we get away from the 'noise' and distractions that life brings, perhaps we can get to a place where we 'listen' to what the future is saying.

In the New Testament Church, one of the primary purposes of the Prophet is to make the church more 'prophetic'. Every believer has the Holy Spirit indwelling within them and possesses the ability of 'hearing His voice'. Therefore, when a Prophet comes and operates, he/she can generally confirm what the Lord has 'already' revealed or bring fresh understanding and perspective. A true prophetic voice speaks from the pages of a book that contains your purposes written and sourced in Heaven. My friends, the Future is speaking.

Are YOU listening?

It is with this question that I begin to extract a life story from the book of Genesis, which I believe serves as a template of prophetic life and calling for the times we currently live in. Let's glean some truths from the life of Joseph, Abraham's Great Grandson.

Dysfunctional Beginnings

Joseph was the twelfth child of a large family living in Canaan. His father Jacob, had two wives (Rachel and Leah) and children from their two maids, Bilhah and Zilpah. Joseph, at the time, was the youngest and the first child of Rachel, whom Jacob truly loved. Consequently, Joseph became Jacob's favourite son.

It is quite interesting how generations of families often repeat the same mistakes. A generation earlier, his father was in a similar situation. As a child, Jacob was his mother's favourite, and his brother, Esau was favoured by his father. This seriously affected the family and because of his mother's favouritism, Jacob had to flee the family household as his brother, Esau sought to kill him.

Joseph is born and raised in a dysfunctional family unit. His father, Jacob, has two wives and four women who bore children for him. Out of the four, only one child was favoured which inevitably leads to tensions within the family unit. The two wives, who happen to be sisters had competed for Jacob's love and attention for years. In an attempt to gain Jacob's favour, Rachel gives her maid over to Jacob and her sister, Leah follows suit with her maid. Both maids give Jacob more children. Four women of two different camps were competing against each other and as a result, children are born within the toxic mix.

Rachel suffered from barrenness for a very long time and had to witness the other women bearing children for her husband and she became very envious of them. Finally, Joseph is born and Jacob is over the moon with joy. His favouritism for Joseph was not hidden and this caused Joseph's siblings to become increasingly resentful of him.

According to the scriptures, Joseph worked in the family business with his brothers. In one instance the brothers were up to no good and Joseph reported them to their father. This intensified their feelings against him and Jacob worsened the situation by gifting Joseph with a special coat of many colours. This blatant sign of favour and love for Joseph alienated the brothers more. The brothers moved from jealousy to hatred and eventually tried to kill Joseph. But, it was in this place of dysfunction that the future begins to speak and Joseph begins to DREAM.

Prophetic Beginnings

At this crucial point, we are going to witness remarkable prophetic revelation from a youngster. The future will speak from a variety of prophetic vehicles with the future coded. This is an area where we all need growth; decoding what the Spirit reveals. The future speaks and Joseph receives messages through a sequence of dreams which marks the beginning of his prophetic development and developmental training. It is a process that took approximately twelve to thirteen years.

The process begins with his first dream:

> Joseph had a dream, and when he told it to his brothers, they hated him all the more. He said to them, 'Listen to this dream I had: we were binding sheaves of corn out in the field when suddenly my sheaf rose and stood upright, while your sheaves gathered round mine and bowed down to it.' His brothers said to him, 'Do you intend to reign over us? Will you actually rule us?' And they hated him all the more because of his dream and what he had said.
> **Genesis 37:5-8**

Soon thereafter he dreams again.

> Then he had another dream, and he told it to his brothers. 'Listen,' he said, 'I had another dream, and this time the sun and moon and eleven stars were bowing down to me.'
>
> When he told his father as well as his brothers, his father rebuked him and said, 'What is this dream you had? Will your mother and I and your brothers actually come and bow down to the ground before you?' His brothers were jealous of him, but his father kept the matter in mind.
> **Genesis 37:9-11**

The future revealed in this dream is coded. With the benefit of hindsight, looking back at the book of Genesis the future that is related in these dreams occurs twelve to thirteen years later when Joseph eventually becomes the prime minister of Egypt. When the future speaks, it uses a variety of prophetic vehicles to do so. In this case a LIFE DREAM deep within Joseph is stirred and activated, pointing not only to his future but to that of his entire family and the region of residence. However, at this time, Joseph is young both in age and prophetic development. We are seeing the birth of the Solutionist, a function in the prophetic that, I believe, will be key in our day. It will mark the onset of our ability to discern and decode the future, along with that of releasing strategy to manage it futuristically.

Prophetic beginnings can be profound sometimes, but we need to remember that it is only the beginning of an evolving process. Joseph's family did not discern what was happening and believed this was the musings of a spoiled young man; even his father scolded him. Although Jacob scolded Joseph, the book of Genesis reveals that Jacob wondered what the dreams meant. After his own prophetic experiences and dreams, Jacob knew something was unusual but he wasn't certain. This serves as a warning for seasoned prophetic people as the language used to communicate in your day may not be the language applied today. The Lord's principles may remain mainly the same but his vehicles and language might change to suit a new generation. We must always remain open or otherwise we may well respond as Jacob did.

The Dream-Killer Assignment

Generally, after your prophetic beginnings, you begin the prophetic process. In these prophetic beginnings, the WHAT and WHY may be revealed to a degree but the process releases the HOW. In other words, the process is the grace of God in operation preparing and training the individual or masses of people for the revealed future. What you discover is that the process is unique and not the same for everyone, as we all have various personality types, character flaws, family or church environments and specific demonic assignments. It is during this critical time that intense spiritual warfare is released and the dream-killer assignment is activated. The dream-killer assignment is simply to kill the dream; to prevent the revealed future from coming to pass. Remember that the purpose for process is preparation. In the realm of the satanic, it is to kill the future.

In Joseph's case, this satanic assignment operates through the family's dysfunction. Jacob's obvious favoritism towards his youngest son opens the door to jealousy and hatred. This soon takes another twist as the hatred reaches the level of murder. While traveling to join his brothers, as his father requested, Joseph was informed that his brothers are in a place called Dothan. They recognized him from a distance wearing the special coat that his father prepared for him and they start conspiring against him.

So Joseph went after his brothers and found them near Dothan. But they saw him in the distance and before he reached them, they plotted to kill him.

> 'Here comes the dreamer!" they said to each other. "Come now let's kill him and throw him into one of the pits and say that a ferocious animal devoured him. Then we we'll see what comes of his dreams.'
> **Genesis 37:17-20**

As we can see, family dysfunction can at times lead to murder. In this case, though, the dream-killer's objective is to kill the focal point of the future which was Joseph himself. "Let's kill his or her dreams" is the objective. When dreaming, be very careful with whom you share the dream or aspirations with because not everyone has the ability to sense the future unfolding in you. Generally, if people are not able to discern or understand it, they WILL come against it. Family, friends or colleagues at times only see you in the light of the past or the present and what people do not understand they generally resist. It is through such people or groups that the dream-killer operates through. Normally it is those closest to you; friends, family or associates.

We see this phenomenon in operation in Jesus' life. In one case, when He was outlining His future.

> 'From that time on Jesus began to explain to his disciples that he must go to Jerusalem and suffer many things at the hand of the elders, chief priests, and teachers of the law and that he must be killed and on the third day be raised to life.
>
> Peter took him aside and began to rebuke Him, 'Never Lord!' he said. 'This shall never happen to you!'
>
> Jesus turned and said to Peter, "Get behind me, Satan! You are a stumbling block to me; you do not have in mind the things of God but the things of men.'
> Matt:16:20-23

At the time, Peter was one of Jesus' disciples; a member of His team touring to spread the Gospel throughout Israel. Moments before Peter received revelation of Jesus' true identity, now he is used by the enemy to express his opinion on a recent revelation regarding Jesus' immediate future. Jesus knew the source of the voice and responded, knowing that the dream-killer was in operation. He immediately engaged in warfare exposing the 'voice' using Peter's mouth. This teaches that we must discern the 'source' of people's opinions and actions when our future is being hindered.

As the brothers began to plan the murder of their brother, they stripped him of his robe and threw Joseph into an empty cistern. While there, his brothers decided against killing him but opted to sell him to Midianite traders on their way to Egypt. To conceal the crime, the brothers concocted a story to tell their father by reporting that Joseph was attacked by a wild animal and killed. In turn, they killed an animal and draped Joseph's robe in blood as evidence to Jacob. The news hit Jacob hard, but Joseph's process had only begun.

CHAPTER FIVE

The Process

If you have a significant Life Dream residing within you, then periods of process are inevitable.

I can only imagine the trauma Joseph must have felt after being sold into slavery by his own brothers. He must have wondered, "what on earth is happening to me". There must have been many times he cried out for deliverance and to be returned home back to the familiar, back to his home and family. However, deliverance didn't come. WHY? Because the process or preparation is the most important and critical time in our lives. Without it, we step into our future unprepared. As tough as it was, this signalled the beginning of the prophetic process in Joseph's life. From my own experience, the process for prophets or leaders appears to be very severe, but it is in the fires of process that something is moulded, which will in turn impact nations. Joseph begins as a slave who entered a nation that he was destined to govern. His process brings him into proximity of the 'world' he is destined to operate within. Once in Egypt, it is initiated when he was sold to Potiphar, a government official. In this regard, he is learning protocol and developing key skills during a critical period.

Pause for a moment... Are you so concerned about your experiences that you cannot discern the 'arena' within which you are destined to operate and have success? Many times, the process period brings us into proximity with the 'arena' in order to acclimate us to it. Regardless of how we got 'there', as in Joseph's case, what's important is that we learn about ourselves and what does and does not work for us. We should learn to identify the skillset needed to operate within our specific 'arena' and what we can bring to the table.

Acclimatisation

Before we continue, I would like to use another biblical account to further my case. Saul was Israel's very first King and was anointed by Samuel, one of Israel's greatest prophetic voices. Although Saul's beginnings were humble, Samuel played a key role in preparing Saul for his future role. Before Saul was anointed King, Samuel was the last of the political/military leaders called Judges. These Judges ruled in the place of Israel's invisible King, who was the Lord Himself. During times of great distress in the nation, the Lord would raise up these Judges (leaders) to lead the nation into freedom. At the time of their meeting, **Samuel** was the leading prophet and operated as a 'Judge' who ruled the nation for many years. While visiting a city within Israel, he was looking for his father's donkeys. Saul was from the tribe of Benjamin, which was the smallest tribe in Israel at the time and belonged to the smallest clan. According to I Samuel, Chapter 9, the day before their meeting, the Lord had informed Samuel that he was going to meet a young man from the tribe of Benjamin. He also told him that this young man would be Israel's first king. Upon meeting Saul, the Lord pointed him out and Samuel begins the acclimation process. God partially introduced Saul to his future and Saul's response indicates that his mind was set on present circumstances. Coming from the smallest tribe and clan had 'conditioned' his mindset to such a degree that when notified of his kingship, he basically said, 'this is where I come from, why are you talking to me like this'?

At that point, Samuel gives Saul a 'taste' of his future by inviting him to participate in the worship celebrations (sacrifices and meal) occurring that day in the city. Upon reaching the 'high place' or shrine, Saul was seated with influential leaders of the city and positioned at the **head** of the table. He was then given the **best** portion of the meal normally reserved for the ruler of the region and began acclimating his mindset towards the future. The next day, Samuel reveals a more detailed account of Saul's immediate future and the rest, as they say, is history. The reason for this interjection is to encourage you to dissuade your mindset from correlating with present circumstances. If you are still going through a process period, understand that you are being prepared for a bigger and brighter future. In revisiting Joseph's story, we are reminded that after working in the family business, his organizational, management and administration skills come to the forefront. He uses them well in Potiphar's house. As they are aligned with the blessing and favour from the Lord, Potiphar takes notice, sees the result of the Lord's favour and promotes him. Meanwhile. Joseph remains faithful and allows his skills to radiate God's glory throughout the process. From slave to personal attendant, Joseph, is now promoted to 'general manager' of Potiphar's entire household. As his responsibilities grow, Joseph's aptitude meets the increasing demands. During this season of his life, it was not the prophetic gift that was being matured but rather his skills and abilities. Joseph's administrative skills and commitment to excellence prepared him for his future role. Essentially, he is training for reigning. The scriptures record that Joseph did his job so well that Potiphar did not worry about anything except what he had to eat or drink.

Dream-Killer Strike Again

At inexplicable times in our lives, satanic assignments can manifest and seemingly frustrate the plan that the Lord has for lives. In Joseph's case, just when it seems things are going well for him, all hell breaks loose. Joseph was a well built and handsome young man and, in doing his job well, Potiphar's wife took a liking to him. Many times, during seasons of promotion, you will get the attention of many, including your enemies. On numerous occasions, she tried to seduce him but out of loyalty to God and his boss, Joseph was relentless. At one point, she finally caught him alone and tried to force herself on him by grabbing his cloak. Joseph had no choice but to run away, leaving his cloak in her hands. After being spurned, she devised a scheming explanation as to why Joseph's cloak was in her possession. The Dream-Killer's assignment always looks for open doors in the people closest to us. It may start with family or the workplace. Lust, fear, insecurity, jealousy, pride, anger, control, rejection and greed are just some of the emotional portals that the Dream Killer operates within. Many good people can be unwittingly used in destroying dreams if these 'doors' remain wide open in their lives.

In Potiphar's wife's case, the door the Dream Killer operated through was lust. Lust or infatuation quickly turned to spite, so she concocted a story accusing Joseph of attempted rape and used his cloak as evidence. When her husband heard of it, he becomes enraged and orders Joseph to prison for a crime he did not commit. Think about it, Joseph passed the test, but he is rewarded with injustice. Even with the best of intentions and operating in integrity, people can misread your actions and inflict damaging blows that can destroy your confidence, self-esteem and integrity. When facing the worst aspects of human nature, especially from those we look up to and trust can end in devastation. Rejection, brokenness and despair experienced during times of despair can seem like a very long and dark prison sentence. We often wonder if we will ever recover. You might be going through something like this right now feeling broken and cast aside. Please know that **you** are the inspiration for this book! If you are living life with a broken heart and shattered dreams, your life and dreams are not over. This is a process and you **will** get through it. How do I know? I have been there and have seen the Grace of God lead me through some very hard times. Trust in His process and be quick to forgive yourself and others. Understand that during your time walking through this fallen world, you **WILL** get hurt, that you **WILL** make mistakes and face enemies/frenemies and people **WILL** disappoint you, but **EVERYTIME** it happens run to the Healer. For He, alone, can take the shattered pieces of our lives and put them back together again!

Like Joseph, your reputation can be trampled in the mud as people will delight in telling lies about you and besmirch your character. You may be falsely accused and misunderstood, be the subject of all types of gossip whether you made a mistake or not. Joseph was put in prison for sexual assault which may have become public knowledge. From such a lofty place, now placed in prison, his reputation was in tatters. Beloved, your process has not finished no matter how low you feel, because deep within you something is still stirring. If your heart is still beating, and you are reading this book then that means you are not **finished** yet! The "fat lady has not sung her last song". Your PURPOSE lives and is approaching a 'Kairos moment' to manifest itself.

Joseph arrives in prison, probably at a very low point in his life. However, the grace of God is with him and in that dark place, Joseph begins to shine. His leadership/management skills become apparent to his jailors. Joseph wins favour with the head jailor and in time, Joseph is running the operations within the jail. When we arrive at low points in our lives, the temptation to 'shut down' can be so compelling as dissipating hope can feel like air leaving a pricked balloon. We often acclimatise to the depressive environment that journeys in life can sometimes take us. It is at these times that the temptation to succumb and 'give up can be so compelling. The inclination to 'stay' in that place becomes very strong but the primary lesson we must learn during these seasons is that 'your' process is about YOU and not necessarily your environment'. YOUR environment will eventually change, and you will move on to the next stage in life. Work with what you have and in due time you will be influencing your 'prison' and not the other way around.

A Shift in Your Gift

The Head Cupbearer and Head Baker, two key officials of Pharaoh's staff are sent to the same prison where Joseph is housed for offending Potiphar. During their time there, they both dream different dreams on the same night. Each of their dreams are so vivid and detailed but they lacked understanding; needing some sort of interpretation. Both men are troubled by their dream. Joseph notices their mood and asks them what is troubling them. They tell him about their dreams and want someone to interpret them. First, the cupbearer relays his dream:

And the chief butler told his dream to Joseph, and said to him, In my dream, behold, a vine was before me;

And in the vine were three branches: and it was as though it budded, and her blossoms shot forth; and the clusters thereof brought forth ripe grapes:

And Pharaoh's cup was in my hand: and I took the grapes, and pressed them into Pharaoh's cup, and I gave the cup into Pharaoh's hand.

And Joseph said unto him, This is the **interpretation** of it
Genesis 40:9-12a

During his time in the process period, Joseph experiences a shift in his gift. As a teenager in Canaan, he had two dreams but did not have the ability to interpret the dreams. However, years later while in prison, Joseph discovers that his gift has shifted to another level. Upon hearing the Head Butler's dream, Joseph demonstrates this new skill and gives a definitive interpretation of the dream.

'The three branches are three days:

Yet within three days shall Pharaoh lift up thine head, and restore thee unto thy place: and thou shalt deliver Pharaoh's cup into his hand, after the former manner when thou wast his butler.
Genesis 40:12-13

The Head Baker is encouraged and shares his dream however Joseph's interpretation of his dream is foreboding as the Baker's life was coming to an end.

I also was in my dream, and, behold, I had three white baskets on my head:

And in the uppermost basket there was of all manner of bakemeats for Pharaoh; and the birds did eat them out of the basket upon my head.

And Joseph answered and said, This, is the interpretation thereof: The three baskets are three days:

Yet within three days shall Pharaoh lift up thy head from off thee, and shall hang thee on a tree; and the birds shall eat thy flesh from off thee.
Genesis 40:17-19

In three days, it would be Pharaoh's birthday and as he celebrated, he reinstated the Head Butler and hung the Head Baker as Joseph predicted. Joseph is now interpreting dreams and giving accurate insight into the future; an ability that would one day take him from the prison to the palace.

Another instance of a shift in gifting is found thousands of years later in the Lord's ministry. Jesus' public ministry is in full swing and his predecessor, John the Baptist is now imprisoned by the designated ruler of Judea, Herod. Jesus and John were not only public leaders of their times but also cousins. The scriptures are not clear on their relationship while they were growing up, but I believe there may have been a few family visits before John started his ministry. According to Matthew 14, the reason Herod arrested John was because John was critical of his marriage to Herodias, his brother's wife. Actually, Herod wanted to kill John but was afraid of public opinion as John was quite popular. While celebrating his birthday, Herodias' daughter is dancing before him and their distinguished guests. Herod is so intoxicated by the performance, he drunkenly made an oath of promise for anything she wants. What he didn't know, was that the young lady was previously encouraged by her mother to ask for John the Baptist's head! So, she asks for John's head to brought to her on a platter. Herod, being afraid of potential embarrassment, orders John to be executed. After burying his body, John's disciples contact Jesus and told him what happened. The news hits hard, as explained before John is not just a forerunner or a contemporary leader; he is FAMILY.

> When Jesus got the news, he slipped away by boat to an out-of-the-way place by himself
> **Matthew 14:13**

This was a direct attack not only on John and his movement but to Jesus as well. He deals with the loss of a loved one amidst his ministry to the public. But, Jesus slipped away to a solitary place, to recover and pray. What was supposed to hinder and momentarily derail the ministry caused a shift in His gift. Jesus found a new and higher level, as later in the chapter two incredible miracles and signs take place. People eventually find out where he is, and they flock to see him. The day wears on, the people are hungry, and this sets the scene for the first of the two previously mentioned miracles.

> And Jesus went forth, and saw a great multitude, and was moved with compassion toward them, and he healed their sick.

> And when it was evening, his disciples came to him, saying, This is a desert place, and the time is now past; send the multitude away, that they may go into the villages, and buy themselves victuals.

> But Jesus said unto them, They need not depart; give ye them to eat.

> And they say unto him, We have here but five loaves, and two fishes.

He said, Bring them hither to me.

And he commanded the multitude to sit down on the grass, and took the five loaves, and the two fishes, and looking up to heaven, he blessed, and brake, and gave the loaves to his disciples, and the disciples to the multitude.

And they did all eat, and were filled: and they took up of the fragments that remained twelve baskets full.

And they that had eaten were about five thousand men, **beside women and children.**
Matthew 14:14-21

A conservative estimate would place 10,000 people in attendance along with five loaves of bread and two pieces of fish. Via a miracle of multiplication, he feeds them all! The second miracle, occurred after the people are sent away with their bellies full. Jesus sent his disciples away on a ship to the other side of the sea and went up the mountain to pray. During the fourth watch (4 am the following morning) a sudden, violent storm occurs. The boat is being battered by the wind and waves. Out of nowhere, Jesus appears walking on water! Now this nothing like the Jim Carey movie 'Bruce Almighty', as Jesus is actually walking on the waves of the sea in amidst the storm.

And in the fourth watch of the night Jesus went unto them, walking on the sea.

And when the disciples saw him walking on the sea, they were troubled, saying, It is a spirit; and they cried out for fear.

But straightway Jesus spake unto them, saying, Be of good
cheer; it is I; be not afraid
Matthew 14:25-27

Time alone with the Father, enabled Him to shift to another level
and will do the same thing for you as well, once you begin to 'see'
adversity for what it really is; a stepping stone to a higher level
instead of a stumbling block. Now referring to Joseph's story, his
process or 'seasoning' hadn't yet finished. After giving the Head
Butler the interpretation to his dream, Joseph asks him not to forget
about him after the Head Butler's release from prison. But the
Butler, once restored to his job, forgets about Joseph who remains
in prison for another two years. But, the dream Joseph had as a
teenager is approaching its appointed time for manifestation.
Prison, in Joseph's life, served to keep and prepare him for this
appointed time. The prophetic begins to stir again and this time
Pharaoh has a dream.

> And it came to pass at the end of two full years, that Pharaoh
> dreamed: and, behold, he stood by the river.
>
> And, behold, there came up out of the river seven well
> favoured kine and fatfleshed; and they fed in a meadow.
>
> And, behold, seven other kine came up after them out of the
> river, ill favoured and leanfleshed; and stood by the other
> kine upon the brink of the river.
>
> And the ill favoured and leanfleshed kine did eat up the
> seven well favoured and fat kine. So Pharaoh awoke.
>
> And he slept and dreamed the second time: and, behold,
> seven ears of corn came up upon one stalk, rank and good.

And, behold, seven thin ears and blasted with the east wind sprung up after them.

And the seven thin ears devoured the seven rank and full ears. And Pharaoh awoke, and, behold, it was a dream.

And it came to pass in the morning that his spirit was troubled; and he sent and called for all the magicians of Egypt, and all the wise men thereof: and Pharaoh told them his dream; but there was none that could interpret them unto Pharaoh.
Genesis 42:1-8

Pharaoh was disturbed by the dreams. As the Leader of the only Super Power and major economy at the time, God was sending him a coded message of the future of his kingdom. A future that would affect the economic outlook of the entire region. The news of Pharaoh's dream came to the ears of the Head Butler. It was then that he remembered Joseph and recommended him to Pharaoh by recounting the events that occurred two years earlier when Joseph accurately interpreted the two dreams.

Pharaoh sent an order for Joseph to be released. After years in prison, Joseph's divine appointment had come, and within a few hours he is out of prison clothes and wearing new garments. He then stood in front of the leader of a nation demanding answers. However, his additional two years in prison led to another shift in his gift as we will begin to see. Pharaoh tells Joseph about the two vivid dreams he had:

And Pharaoh said unto Joseph, I have dreamed a dream, and there is none that can interpret it: and I have heard say of thee, that thou canst understand a dream to interpret it.

And Joseph answered Pharaoh, saying, It is not in me: God shall give Pharaoh an answer of peace.

And Pharaoh said unto Joseph, In my dream, behold, I stood upon the bank of the river:

And, behold, there came up out of the river seven kine, fatfleshed and well favoured; and they fed in a meadow:

And, behold, seven other kine came up after them, poor and very ill favoured and leanfleshed, such as I never saw in all the land of Egypt for badness:

And the lean and the ill favoured kine did eat up the first seven fat kine:

And when they had eaten them up, it could not be known that they had eaten them; but they were still ill favoured, as at the beginning. So I awoke.

And I saw in my dream, and, behold, seven ears came up in one stalk, full and good:

And, behold, seven ears, withered, thin, and blasted with the east wind, sprung up after them:

And the thin ears devoured the seven good ears: and I told this unto the magicians; but there was none that could declare it to me.

Genesis 42:15-24

Joseph immediately discerned that the two dreams, although different, conveyed the same message. He told Pharaoh that God was revealing to him and his government, what was in store for the FUTURE of the region. A FUTURE coded even from psychics and magicians that only Joseph could interpret. While interpreting the dream, Joseph said that the initial seven cattle and seven ears of grain in the first dream, represents the next seven years of the region's or kingdom's economy. He predicted seven years of great abundance. However, the thin cows and thin seven ears of grain, signaled a pending seven-year period of famine slated to begin after the seven years of abundance. This famine would be so severe that all of the prosperity of the previous seven years would be used up and forgotten. Hence, Pharaoh and his cabinet were given insight into the economic cycle for the next fourteen years. Think about that for a moment... the major superpower or nation in that region knew what was coming and had exclusive knowledge into the future based on Joseph's interpretation.

It is in this moment, we see why Joseph was left in prison two full years after the Head Butler had been reinstated; there was a new shift in his gifting! Two more years of process and seasoning produced something unseen in Joseph's life prior to this. As a teenager, he dreamed. In the prison he interpreted, but in Pharaoh's presence, Joseph moves into an arena called FUTURE MANAGEMENT. The next 14-year cycle is revealed, a solution and strategy borne from 'the Spirit of Wisdom' and Joseph's managerial/administrative skills are offered to Pharaoh. In effect, Joseph is saying to the government of his day, this is the FUTURE and this is how you MANAGE it.

Now therefore let Pharaoh look out a man discreet and wise, and set him over the land of Egypt.

Let Pharaoh do this, and let him appoint officers over the land, and take up the fifth part of the land of Egypt in the seven plenteous years.

And let them gather all the food of those good years that come, and lay up corn under the hand of Pharaoh, and let them keep food in the cities.

And that food shall be for store to the land against the seven years of famine, which shall be in the land of Egypt; that the land perish not through the famine.
Genesis 41:34-36

Pharaoh was so impressed with what he heard and listened keenly to the advice that Joseph gave him. He decided at that divine moment that there was one man for the job. A young prophetic Hebrew who had spent his whole life in preparation for such a time as this. The Message Bible captures the moment below:

This seemed like a good idea to Pharaoh and his officials.

Then Pharaoh said to his officials, "**Isn't this the man we need?** Are we going to find anyone else who has God's spirit in him like this?"

So Pharaoh said to Joseph, "**You're the man for us. God has given you the inside story**—no one is as qualified as you in experience and wisdom. From now on, you're in charge of my affairs; all my people will report to you. Only as king will I be over you."

So Pharaoh commissioned Joseph: "I'm putting you in charge of the entire country of Egypt." Then Pharaoh removed his signet ring from his finger and slipped it on Joseph's hand. He outfitted him in robes of the best linen and put a gold chain around his neck. He put the second-in-command chariot at his disposal, and as he rode people shouted "Bravo!"

Genesis 41:38-43

Joseph became the prime minister of a nation he entered as a slave and is tasked to FUTURE MANAGE the nation for the next 14-year cycle. Implementing his strategies would mean that Egypt would be saved from the devastating famine AND would retain and maximise its economic advantage in the region. In these current times, generations are crying out for 'the solutionist'. Crying out for individuals or a people group who can not only discern the future, but also teach strategies to manage it. Imagine being at the head of a company knowing future trends or how the market is going to function for the next 14 years. That level of insight is priceless. I believe that level of insight is both available and waiting to be accessed. The prophetic is aimed at individual people, people groups, places, things, cities, regions and nations. Each unit has an assigned future waiting to be revealed and discovered. Without process, Joseph would not have been ready for this divine appointment and become one of the most revered leaders of his time. Every life story is different, and the years or methods of process are unique to the individual. The process is an essential part of preparation that equips us for our FUTURE and the people that we are destined to impact.

CHAPTER SIX

The Kingdom –
The FutureNow Template

The Bible is not only considered the 'Holy Book' that predicts what happens at the end of the age, other books such as the Koran do so as well. One thing they all agree on, though, is that in the future a very charismatic leader will come and set in place one common political/economic system and unite the religions of the world. Where they differ is who this leader is. When reading the prophetic books of the Bible, clearly people, organizations and nations are heading towards a FUTURE prepared for them. The FUTURE can be defined as "a time-based reality not yet experienced". It is something that simply cannot be avoided. One way or another, the FUTURE is coming.

Regarding the book of Revelation contained in the Bible, while 'uncovering Jesus Christ and who He is', it reveals the future of three major people groups. The Gentiles (non-Jews), the Jewish people and lastly the church. It also describes the judgement coming to the world and its systems. The book reveals an age where evil and every enemy has triumphed and the dawning of a new age: A time where every tear is wiped away and a new era begins with Heaven on Earth where there is no evil or suffering under the Kingship of Jesus. Daniel also saw this period of the FUTURE. The pre-eminent Kingdom of his day, Babylon, was fully in it's pomp with

Nebuchadnezzar as king. In a similar situation to Pharaoh of Egypt, Nebuchadnezzar dreams and it disturbs him. He knows the dream conveys an important message but simply can't interpret it. Eventually, Daniel, after a period of fasting and prayer, provided insight into the King's dream. He then interprets the dream and in doing so, uncovers the FUTURE:

> Thou, O king, sawest, and behold a great image. This great image, whose brightness was excellent, stood before thee; and the form thereof was terrible.

> This image's head was of fine gold, his breast and his arms of silver, his belly and his thighs of brass,

> His legs of iron, his feet part of iron and part of clay.

> Thou sawest till that a stone was cut out without hands, which smote the image upon his feet that were of iron and clay, and brake them to pieces.

> Then was the iron, the clay, the brass, the silver, and the gold, broken to pieces together, and became like the chaff of the summer threshing floors; and the wind carried them away, that no place was found for them: and the stone that smote the image became a great mountain, and filled the whole earth

> This is the dream; and we will tell the interpretation thereof before the king.

> Thou, O king, art a king of kings: for the God of heaven hath given thee a kingdom, power, and strength, and glory.

And wheresoever the children of men dwell, the beasts of the field and the fowls of the heaven hath he given into thine hand, and hath made thee ruler over them all. Thou art this head of gold.

And after thee shall arise another kingdom inferior to thee, and another third kingdom of brass, which shall bear rule over all the earth.

And the fourth kingdom shall be strong as iron: forasmuch as iron breaketh in pieces and subdueth all things: and as iron that breaketh all these, shall it break in pieces and bruise.

And whereas thou sawest the feet and toes, part of potters' clay, and part of iron, the kingdom shall be divided; but there shall be in it of the strength of the iron, forasmuch as thou sawest the iron mixed with miry clay.

And as the toes of the feet were part of iron, and part of clay, so the kingdom shall be partly strong, and partly broken.

And whereas thou sawest iron mixed with miry clay, they shall mingle themselves with the seed of men: but they shall not cleave one to another, even as iron is not mixed with clay.

And in the days of these kings shall the God of heaven set up a kingdom, which shall never be destroyed: and the kingdom shall not be left to other people, but it shall break in pieces and consume all these kingdoms, and it shall stand for ever. Daniel 2:31-35

Daniel shows Nebuchadnezzar the future. After his kingdom, the Medes-Persians become the dominant kingdom and then the Greeks through Alexander the Great emerge. Afterwards, the Roman Empire rises to prominence and then a future kingdom is symbolized by "feet with toes that were partly iron and partly clay". These ten toes are the same number of horns that both Daniel and John see on a beast/dragon in their respective prophetic discourses. These horns represent 10 nations or kings that will give up their rule to the Anti-Christ at some point in the future. Now between the Roman Empire and these future kingdoms, Father institutes His OWN Kingdom. This Kingdom of Heaven is represented by a stone being cut with invisible hands. This stone strikes this awesome image on its feet, causing it to fall and break into pieces. Pieces of gold, silver, iron and miry clay are then swept away and the 'stone' grows into a great mountain that fills all of the earth. A new age dawns and the Kingdom of Heaven rules and dominates the entire Earth. This Kingdom will never be destroyed and is destined to consume, destroy and outlast all the other kingdoms represented by the great image. This future and present reality was Jesus' reference point at the very start of his ministry. The law of first mention comes into play here, as the message of the Kingdom is the major theme of his ministry.

> From that time Jesus began to preach, and to say, Repent: for the kingdom of heaven is at hand.
> Matthew 4:17

Most Jews at the time had a working knowledge of the Messiah and His Kingdom. However, Jesus was effectively saying that this future reality/ dominion was immediately accessible through repentance. While preaching the message of the Kingdom, many were healed, delivered from demonic bondages; miracles and signs and wonders occurred. The FUTURE coming Kingdom was making a dramatic entrance into the Earth through its King, and the very rule of Heaven came to Earth through the Lord's Christ. Jesus' ministry, life, death and resurrection was designed to give His Father the legal right to destroy evil in our world once and for all through this same Kingdom. Looking at history, we know that Jesus lived during the prominence of the Roman Empire, Judea at the point in time was under Roman rule operating primarily through King Herod who ruled the client state and Pontius Pilate, the governor of Judea. The Sanhedrin governed religious and civil matters but It would be fair to say that the machinations of the rule of Rome was dominant in that region. To take this thought further, Rome in it's pomp was ruled by Caesar and governed their territories through what is called a senate. A group of called out one's chosen to represent Caesar in their respective territories and also to represent their territories to their Caesar. This form of governing was what Jesus knew about firsthand. In describing the establishing of His own Kingdom, Jesus uses governmental terminology not an ecclesiastical one. The Father was never interested in just setting up a religious order, He desires to transform the WHOLE Earth back to it's original design and function and has chosen the KINGDOM through His church as His vehicle to do so.

When Jesus arrived in the villages of Caesarea Philippi, he asked his disciples, "What are people saying about who the Son of Man is?"

They replied, "Some think he is John the Baptizer, some say Elijah, some Jeremiah or one of the other prophets."

He pressed them, "And how about you? Who do you say I am?"

Simon Peter said, "You're the Christ, the Messiah, the Son of the living God."

Jesus came back, "God bless you, Simon, son of Jonah! You didn't get that answer out of books or from teachers. My Father in heaven, God himself, let you in on this secret of who I really am. And now I'm going to tell you who you are, really are. You are Peter, a rock. This is the rock on which I will put together my church, a church so expansive with energy that not even the gates of hell will be able to keep it out.

"And that's not all. You will have complete and free access to God's kingdom, keys to open any and every door: no more barriers between heaven and earth, earth and heaven. A yes on earth is yes in heaven. A no on earth is no in heaven."
Matthew 16:13-18 (Message Bible)

I have used the Message version of this text purposely, as it fully outlines the points being made in this chapter of the book. The word church here is translated from the Greek word 'Ecclesia' which again is a political term not a religious one. The ancient Greeks ruled through an ecclesia (assembly) made up of male citizens over the age of 30 years old. It was a political system of governing that birthed what we call today 'democracy'. However, it was slightly different from the democracy that exists in our day, as there was only ONE party not two or three. Today we vote for a particular political party or ideology, back then the 'assembly voted' on civil matters and respective legislation that would effect the whole nation or state. The Romans when they emerged, further developed this idea in their Empire and ruled through a Senate. Again called out or summoned individuals that made political decisions on behalf of

Caesar. The reason why Jesus called the church 'My Church' was simply because there were other systems of governance operating at the time and as the King of His Kingdom, he was setting up His own. An Assembly has the following definition 'as a group of people gathered together in one place for a common purpose'. The church is an assembly of people or a community that is called out to represent King Jesus and His Kingdom in their respective territories. The church has been commissioned to preach the Gospel of the Kingdom to all nations and to disciple them. The Gospel, in essence, is the announcement of the King and His Kingdom coming to all the nations.

Invisible Warfare

Now before we take this thought to the next stages, we need to understand the significance of the above statement and where it was made. Caesarea, Philippi was at least a twelve hours journey from where Jesus was operating his ministry in Southern Israel. The city now is in Northern Israel in the Golan Heights and is current known as Banias. Banias is a lush place and is located at the southern western base of Mount Hermon, It is adjacent to a huge wall of rock, with a cave that is an entrance to a huge spring that is a source of water for the Jordan River. Banias also used to be known as Panias which begins to give an insight into it's history. After the United Kingdom of Israel was split into two due to internal tensions under King Solomon, the Northern Kingdom fell into idolatry, and worshipped an entity called Baal. A system of worship that was prominent in the Middle East at the time. In doing so they set up shrines for Baal. This great wall of rock in the city was used to do so and was known as the 'Rock of the gods'. In Jesus' time, the city was renamed Caesarea but was dedicated to the worship of 'Pan' the half goat and half man Greek deity and people believed that Pan actually lived in the cave embedded in the rock. Pan was a deity associated with every conceivable sexual immorality and a grotto was made for the 'worship' activities. The city was a centre for Pagan worship and shrines were built dedicated to 'Pan'. According to history, Herod Philip rebuilt the city and erected two big temples there, one dedicated to Caesar Augustus and the other to the Greek god, Zeus. One thing to note, is that these worshipped entities remained but their 'packaging' and branding had and still continually changes. As mentioned before, in the Middle East, Baal worship was the main system of worship. To get further understanding, we need to go way back in time and revisit the book of Genesis. Chapter 11 give us some insight into this system of worship. Soon after the flood in Noah times this system of worship was devised by the very first Empire under a leader called Nimrod. He was the prototype 'Caesar' of his day and not only ruled over his subjects but demanded their worship. He introduced this system of governance and the state religion, where there was One King, One language and One religion. It was this system that devised the ill advised plan to build the tower of Babel. God intervened by creating new languages and thwarted their plans. Up until this time, people gathered in one place but as the new languages were created the population scattered and new nations were formed associated by language. However, this system of worship remained and the focal point of worship had different names as a result of Heaven's intervention. In the Middle East,the head or premier 'god' was called Baal, to the Greeks he was called Zeus and to the Romans he was called Jupiter. This same entity had differing names depending on the region where this worship system operated. Evil doesn't go away but with each successive generation, it finds new ways/methods of expression.

Now the cave dedicated to 'Pan' was known as the 'Gates of Hades'. The Greeks and the Romans considered it a portal for the underworld where spiritual entities would traverse through. A place of great spiritual power, where both Romans and Greeks used to get 'revelations' of the future from these same entities. Just to take this point further These 'entities' are the unseen evil that motivated the successive Empires and continue to operate in our day. A great example of this is the rise of the Nazis and Adolf Hitler in the last century which sparked World War 2. In History, we tend to focus on the political and socio-economic conditions that gave rise to the 'Fuhrer' but something else took place in Germany a few years prior that can at least explain the darkness that obscured the nation at the time. A German engineer called Carl Humann began the process of bringing an ancient artefact from the city of Pergamum to Berlin called the 'Alter of Zeus' in the 19th Century. This artefact was reassembled in Berlin and a whole museum was dedicated to it. Called the 'Museum of Pergamum'. The Alter was known as a throne for Zeus in one of the most influential cities in the Roman Empire at the time. In a message to the church in Pergamum in the book of Revelation, Jesus reveals the true nature of Zeus and says the following.

> 'I know where you live—where Satan has his throne. Yet you remain true to my name. You did not renounce your faith in me, not even in the days of Antipas, my faithful witness, who was put to death in your city—where Satan lives.'
> **Revelation 2:13**

This Altar is described as 'Satan's Throne' and in the early part of the twentieth century, these stones are reassembled. What the Germans didn't know was that a supernatural 'Gateway' was now opened in their region. Within a few short years after this, Germany and Europe are plunged into a darkness that killed millions of people during both World Wars 1 and 2. The twentieth century despite the technological advances is the most bloodiest century on record. The amount of lives lost in war or murdered by their own state reached new highs. As previously mentioned, Babylon, the Greeks and the Roman Empire had similar 'deities' empowering their kingdoms. Adolf Hitler and his National Socialist Party were no different. Hitler and his leaders were inspired by the occult and it is widely known that he took inspiration from this remodelled temple and constructed buildings in Nuremberg, Germany where he had many of his infamous rallies. The bible in Ephesians 6 describes and categorizes these invisible entities that influence and find expression through culture, the law and politics etc. Today, there's indescribable evil taking place, and it is sourced by these beings manipulating the human heart causing suffering to so many.

For we wrestle not against flesh and blood, but against principalities, against powers, against the rulers of the darkness of this world, against spiritual wickedness in high places.

Wherefore take unto you the whole armour of God, that ye may be able to withstand in the evil day, and having done all, to stand.
Ephesians 6:12-13

When Jesus came to Caesarea Philippi as described in Matthew Chapter 16, he came to confront the 'gates of Hades' operating in his region in person and send a Kingdom Decree to those gates. Notice gates don't move, they are stationary in nature. He (Jesus) took his disciples to the 'Gates of Hell/Hades' in full view of the dedicated temples and 'supernatural engine' sourcing the evil in His region. He went on to make a declaration of war to the realm invisible. Jesus went to the 'gates' and announced His and Heaven's intentions. This shows a mindset that needs to be adopted by His assembly today especially in these times. Decrees full of revelation from Heaven need to be made against the 'gate of hades' operating in our respective regions. One thing I love about this account is it's simplicity and profoundness. The rock and the gates were not just metaphors but things that were visual for His disciples to actually see. His disciples were told that these' gates of hades' would not prevail against them and that they had access to His Kingdom, the very source of His authority on Earth. Shortly after His death, resurrection and ascension these disciples are sent out with the gospel of His Kingdom to start this new movement from Jerusalem. This Kingdom movement has spread and has grown to influence the whole world. In contrast, the system of the worship of Zeus, Pan and Caesar hardly exist at all. If we (His Assembly) become a movement we were originally intended to be, instead of being a religious monument then we too can and will face down and defeat the present evil and structures in our day.

The Gospel of The Kingdom – A FutureNow Reality

The Gospel is translated from the Greek word 'Euangelion'. In this sense it is the announcement of a new King who has recently conquered a given TERRITORY and has established His rule there. As previously mentioned in this chapter, it is also the announcement or the good news of the reign of King Jesus and His Kingdom. This Kingdom designed to manifest itself at the end of this age is available and accessible NOW. We are all invited, by this King Himself to leave our old way of living and transfer our allegiances to Him and experience the realities of His Kingdom now. King Jesus and His Kingdom are the ultimate FutureNow reality. From the beginning of time, the Kingdom was gradually revealed until the time of His arrival. He taught a new way of living, a way of life not governed by this evil age in which we live but by this invisible realm of love, glory, power and authority. He will in the coming FUTURE take up His Rule from the city of Jerusalem. When King Jesus comes at that point in time, He is bringing the RULE of Heaven on Earth and all nations will be subservient to Him. The Gospel of the Kingdom invites everyone to participate with Him and increase the influence of His Kingdom in our lives NOW. By doing so, we allow Heaven and the FUTURE direct access to 'touch' our world.

The decision to make this same Jesus to become Lord is not just a 'religious' one. It is an invitation to join His assembly, to walk with Him and be used as an 'Agent of Change' to influence and transform EVERY part of our world. It is an invitation open to you NOW. If you are reading this book and don't know the Christ/Messiah or have just grown complacent in your walk, why not take a moment to change. Turn away from your current lifestyle, say sorry for the things you have done to offend Him. Recognise what He endured during His crucifixion paying the ultimate price for us all and why He did it. To ensure that you and I could have direct access to the Father. Invite this wonderful King to take leadership in your life and I promise your life will never be the same.

CHAPTER SEVEN

Quantum Leadership

Quantum Leadership is defined as' the process of leading from the future'. The question to ask is what dimension of time are we, as a 'Kingdom Community', leading from.

I would like to go back and look again at Abraham's story to take this point further. As explained in previous chapters, Abraham arrived into Canaan with a promise that the region would be given to his descendants forever. Think about this for a moment, the future direction for the land of Canaan was residing IN one man and his family. None of the inhabitants or rulers at that time knew how the region would ultimately change, except Abraham. Before we get into the nuts and bolts of quantum leadership, Genesis Chapter 18 gives us some insight into how the Father operates. Abraham has an unusual visitation from the Lord. Three men turn up at Abraham's tent and one of them is the Lord Himself. As explained in Chapter 3, the Lord informs Abraham of Isaac's impending birth fulfilling a promise made 24 years earlier. However, another reason for this visitation is revealed. The cities of Sodom and Gomorrah had fallen into such a degree of moral decay that a 'sound' had been released that caught Heaven's attention. The city had become so lawless that the suffering of the innocent sent out a powerful outcry that Heaven demanded justice. Father operates in sound; the Earth and all matter has sound waves within them because they were 'SPOKEN' into being. Sin, injustice within a nation, city or region according to this chapter, sends an OUTCRY to Heaven and when it becomes too severe it invites and incurs judgement.

> Then the Lord said, "The outcry against Sodom and Gomorrah is so great and their sin so grievous that I will go down and see if what they have done is as bad as the outcry that has reached me. If not, I will know."
> **Genesis 18:20-21**

The LORD came down to inspect and see if the city was as bad as or MEASURED up to the 'OUTCRY' He heard. Measuring is another aspect of the Lord's dealings with humanity. A measuring rod was used to measure the temple in Ezekiel's vision. Noah's Ark and the Tabernacle of Moses was made in accordance to strict measurements. At certain seasons He inspects and measures if things are as He intends them to be. With Sodom and Gomorrah at that time, the city was being inspected and measured using the outcry that had gone to Heaven and was found wanting. Here is a powerful lesson for leaders, intercessors and emerging prophetic voices. Even the suffering that sin brings incurs an outcry that demands justice and judgement from Heaven. In this instance, the second nuanced reason for Abraham's visitation is revealed. Father desired to hear another sound, that of intercession. Sometimes when entering His Presence, you have to discern the Lord's mood. Yes, He does have moods and discerning His mood will help us partner with Heaven more effectively. Abraham discerned His mood and immediately started to pray, Genesis Chapter 18 records the following:

The men turned away and went toward Sodom, but Abraham remained standing before the Lord.[d] Then Abraham approached him and said: "Will you sweep away the righteous with the wicked? What if there are fifty righteous people in the city? Will you really sweep it away and not spare[e] the place for the sake of the fifty righteous people in it? Far be it from you to do such a thing—to kill the righteous with the wicked, treating the righteous and the wicked alike. Far be it from you! Will not the Judge of all the earth do right?"

Genesis 18:23-25

In full view of the impending judgement on this city, the Lord actively seeks out His friend to hear the Sound of Intercession that could potentially limit the effects of this judgement and loss of life: A Sound that can release undeserved mercy on these cities. In response to Abraham's intercession, the Lord responds, His Mercy reaches out despite His anger at the suffering in the city. He promises Abraham that the city won't be destroyed if FIFTY righteous people are found within. Now I don't have a census that would tell us how many people lived there but a conservative estimate could be at least 500 to 1,000 people. The chapter reveals that Abraham continues to intercede and the number goes down considerably to 10 people. If Sodom and Gomorrah had ten righteous people within it, at that point in time, it may have survived. However, the city was ultimately destroyed with only six survivors which included Lot (Abraham's nephew). When the innocent suffer, it releases an Outcry that rises to Heaven and DEMANDS justice. There are so many examples of when impending judgement is about to befall an individual, people group, city or nation that the Father seeks someone who will INTERCEDE.

Isaiah Chapter 59, highlights the moral decay of the nation of Israel and in the following verses shows the Lord's response:

> Then the Lord saw it, and it displeased Him
> That there was no justice.
> He saw that there was no man,
> And wondered that there was no intercessor;
> Isaiah 59:15-16

Intercessors continue to release a sound on behalf of your family, city and nation as the Lord is actively 'seeking you out' to stand in and fill the void between judgement and mercy.

Your Revealed Future Releases Present Day Insights

In terms of Quantum Leadership, Father leads from your future not necessarily from your present. Further analysis of this chapter reveals something quite profound. Just before the Lord reveals what He intends to do in the region, the writer of Genesis is given access to the Lord's thoughts at this moment:

> And the Lord said, Shall I hide from Abraham that thing which I do;
>
> Seeing that Abraham shall surely become a great and mighty nation, and all the nations of the earth shall be blessed in him?
>
> For I know him, that he will command his children and his household after him, and they shall keep the way of the Lord, to do justice and judgment; that the Lord may bring upon Abraham that which he hath spoken of him.
> Genesis 18:17-19

While sitting in front of Abraham and receiving his hospitality, the Father decides that He cannot keep His intentions in the region a secret, because He sees something special about Abraham. He sees his FUTURE as a reality. You see at that point in time, Isaac hasn't been conceived or born but was in the realm of the PROMISE. Being in that moment, Abraham's future, although not in existence, was a reality that the Father saw. Father dealt with Abraham in full view of his future when He revealed what He was about to do in relation to Sodom and Gomorrah. As a result, he couldn't HIDE what He intended to do in the region. Beloved, when the Father looks at you right now, He is dealing with you in correlation to your FUTURE. There are things He cannot hide from you due to what He SEES. There may be promises that you haven't seen yet in your life, just like Abraham, but YOUR future remains a reality to Him even now. He sees you in light of what His SON accomplished with His life, death, resurrection and ascension. He also sees your redeemed FUTURE. This can explain why, at many times, while at our worst, the Father continues to behave the way He does by guiding us on into a future He has so lovingly prepared.

One example of this stands out for me in the transformation of a young man of seventeen, who was spiritually lost and angry with no hope of a future. Amidst challenging teenage years, stood on the cusp of street life. As the first born child to Jamaican immigrants, he was the product of a dysfunctional family unit along with the challenging socio-economic environment of the 1980's. Race relations were at an all-time low in the United Kingdom. Why? Because that was the first generation of the immigrants who arrived in the Sixties and simply refused to suffer the levels of racism that their parents endured. This resulted in one of the most turbulent times in British history. Life and the environment sucked out every sense of hope, as society and educational systems instilled low expectations based on the colour of his skin. In the backdrop of all of this, a church in North West London was experiencing an intense prophetic presence when a word is released that Apostles and Prophets from their midst would be raised and released into the nations. Little would anyone realise that one of these would be that lost young man, who at the time had no idea what his destiny would be. The Father saw him through the lens of His Son and the reality of his future began a process that took him on a journey that ultimately enabled this young man to empower and impact many others in different nations. Soon after this prophetic word, this young man had a radical encounter with Jesus and within a few short years, began operating in the prophetic, healing and miracles. That young man, as you have probably guessed is me, the author of this book. I don't know where you are right now but there is no mistake or situation that can erase His love for you or the reality of YOUR FUTURE. You might not know about it or see it right now, but there is ONE who does and He is inviting you to join Him on an adventure that will take you into a FUTURE you were BORN for.

Faith

An important aspect of FutureNow Living is developing Quantum Leadership and learning the process of leading from the future. While comparing Himself to man-made idols and false gods of Babylon, Father says something very interesting.

> Remember the former things of old: for I am God, and there is none else; I am God, and there is none like me,

> Declaring the end from the beginning, and from ancient times the things that are not yet done, saying, My counsel

shall stand, and I will do all my pleasure:'
Isaiah 46: 9-10

One of the things that make Him who He is is the ability to call the 'end from the beginning' or in this context the FUTURE from the present. As One who exists outside of time, space and matter and lives in Eternity, the future is known and is on many occasions declared before it manifests in time. In Genesis Chapter 12, Father invites Abraham through the vehicle of a prophetic word to see his future right in the midst of his present circumstances. Sometimes when the future speaks it makes no sense to the present. Abraham's present at that point was that his wife was barren and he lived in another country but the FUTURE speaks. It informs him that he will become a great nation, inherit a country and be a blessing to all the future families on earth.

If I travelled back 35 years in time and started mentioning the name Facebook, Twitter, the internet or Social Media, it wouldn't make any sense to anyone alive in 1984. The end of a story never correlates to the beginning. The start of your journey in life, is just that, a start, but ONLY One knows how it is going to end. Being the Communicator that HE is, He loves to open our eyes to a future He designed in Eternity. He does this by placing our future within us and giving us the time to discover it. He uses the medium of the Prophetic to 'activate' what has been placed inside of us to enable us to see what 'THERE' (the future) looks like.

Lessons from the life of Abraham, the Father of Faith, can assist us in allowing the revealed future (THERE) to shape our thinking and behaviour. A lifestyle of faith is a prerequisite that gives this revealed future access to our present. The chapter, The Language of Faith, goes into more detail regarding Abraham's journey of faith (please read to recap). We discovered that faith not only helps us connect to the things that are supernatural (unseen), but also connects us to the future. However, another language that we need to discover and learn is 'the language of the Spirit'. Father is so multi-dimensional and lives and operates outside of 'time' as we know it. Even though He communicates to us in our native tongue, His language is different. Why? Because He speaks FUTURE NOW. Almost everything He says relates to where we are (the present) and is loaded with the FUTURE. Once that word is spoken and received, faith for the future is deposited in the heart of the hearer. Why?? To regulate the hearer to live in accordance with the future instead of the present. A practical example of this can be seen with athletes training for the Olympics. Their training regimen is designed to get them ready to perform in the 'future' when the Olympics begins. In other words the future is making it's impact by adjusting the present behaviour and lifestyle of these athletes.

So, Abraham's insight into the future fuelled his faith. Without a level of this type of insight, faith cannot be lived. The unseen must be known and seen in order to live by faith. Even though the Old Testament reveals Abraham 'saw' his future in terms of the land he would inherit and the knowledge that His descendants would become a great nation, the New Testament shows us that Abraham saw much more of the future than initially realized. While confronting the religious Jews who were opposing Him at the time, Jesus said this:

> 'Your father Abraham rejoiced to see my day: and he saw it, and was glad. KJV
> **John 8:56**

In fact, the writer of the book of Hebrews takes this thought even further. Chapter 11 of that book, highlights what faith is and describes how the lifestyle of faith impacted the lives of some of the prominent individuals in the Old Testament. It reveals how the future revealed fuelled their faith. Verse 8 of this Chapter discloses something mind-blowing. It demonstrates that Abraham saw more of the future:

> By an act of faith, Abraham said yes to God's call to travel to an unknown place that would become his home. When he left he had no idea where he was going. By an act of faith he lived in the country promised him, lived as a stranger camping in tents. Isaac and Jacob did the same, living under the same promise. Abraham did it by keeping his eye on an unseen city with real, eternal foundations—the City designed and built by God. MSG
> **Hebrews 11: 8-10**

Which city is the writer of Hebrews talking about?? The answer is revealed in the book of Revelation. The Apostle John sees the future; an age where sin, death and related sufferings are no more. A city coming out of Heaven which was designed and built by God. John sees the very city that Abraham kept his eye on, while living in Israel with Isaac and his grandchildren so many years ago. Abraham saw the dawning of the age to come.

> Then I saw "a new heaven and a new earth,"[a] for the first heaven and the first earth had passed away, and there was no longer any sea. 2 I saw the Holy City, the new Jerusalem, coming down out of heaven from God, prepared as a bride beautifully dressed for her husband. 3 And I heard a loud voice from the throne saying, "Look! God's dwelling place is

now among the people, and he will dwell with them. They will be his people, and God himself will be with them and be their God. 4 'He will wipe every tear from their eyes. There will be no more death'[b] or mourning or crying or pain, for the old order of things has passed away." NIV

Revelation 21: 1-4

Abraham kept his eye on the future. This future reality governed his life and the way he led his family. Quantum Leadership isn't just for entrepreneur's and corporations, it was meant for ordinary people like you and me to lead our families into what the Lord has promised us. Faith is a key component in enabling us to do so.

A Heavenly Blue Print

For the 'Ecclesia' King Jesus' Assembly on Earth, quantum leadership is a must. If the church is a kingdom community, then the will of the King in Heaven trumps every agenda. As mentioned previously in Chapter 6 of this book, His Assembly is the primary vehicle for getting the Will of Heaven accomplished here on Earth. To build or do something of any significance, a plan or blueprint is needed. That blueprint is revealed in the vision/dream of an individual, people group or organisation. It is the future revealed in your vision/dream that the Father wants to use to transform our society. In order to begin the transformation process a clear view of 'there' or the revealed future must be seen and known. Quantum leadership is the process of leading from wherever or whatever 'there' is. The place 'There' in this context is that point in the future that the vision and dream relates to. It is the DESTINATION that needs to be reached. It is the ultimate point of reference for any decisions made in the PRESENT. It is what your current management systems should be based upon. According to the Bible, in the book of Ephesians, the Father already has plans for the fulness of times and through the wonders of the New Covenant, has invested some of those plans in His Sons and Daughters. The challenge of this book is to activate those Eternal plans for our lives and our cities that are lying dormant within.

Redemptive Giftings

Every individual or group has what is called a redemptive gift. It is an innate ability to be resourceful and a blessing to others. This is also true of cities, regions and nations. There is spiritual DNA in every city and nation that directly relates to its people and resources found within the land itself. The prophetic discourse for the seven churches in the 2nd & 3rd Chapters of the Book of Revelation provides insight. There is a lot of conjecture regarding the messages sent to these churches and their interpretation relating to today. I am going to single out the message to the Church in Laodicea in Chapter 3.

"To the angel of the church in Laodicea write:

These are the words of the Amen, the faithful and true witness, the ruler of God's creation. I know your deeds, that you are neither cold nor hot. I wish you were either one or the other! So, because you are lukewarm—neither hot nor cold—I am about to spit you out of my mouth. You say, 'I am rich; I have acquired wealth and do not need a thing.' But you do not realize that you are wretched, pitiful, poor, blind and naked. I counsel you to buy from me gold refined in the fire, so you can become rich; and white clothes to wear, so you can cover your shameful nakedness; and salve to put on your eyes, so you can see.

Those whom I love I rebuke and discipline. So be earnest and repent. Here I am! I stand at the door and knock. If anyone hears my voice and opens the door, I will come in and eat with that person, and they with me.
Revelation 3:14-20

Many times, this message is given a spiritual explanation but the prophetic word also speaks into the DNA of the city. First of all, the source of the Laodicean water supply were hot springs located five miles outside of the city. An aqueduct brought the water from the hot springs to the city and by the time it arrived into the city, it was tepid; neither cold or hot. Another instance is mentioned in Verse 17, where it says 'You say, I am rich'. Laodicea was a financial and banking centre within the Roman Empire and was based in modern-day Turkey in the Denizli province. Additionally, the encouragement to buy eyesalve also speaks to the DNA of the city. Laodicea had a medical centre where a famous ophthalmologist operated. Lastly, the city lay within the region of Phrygia, where ingredients of eye lotions were believed to have originated. There is no doubt that the message to the church in Laodicea included a clear rebuke and instructions to rectify their shortcomings. However, employing the use of certain words reinforced the essence of what was being said to the first century believers at that time. Another key point of the messages to the seven churches is that there were seven distinct prophetic words for seven churches in seven separate locations. In the realm of the prophetic there isn't a one size fits all concept. In other words, a Word for New York would not be the same as a WORD for Paris. Two different cities, with differing spiritual DNA and destinies.

As with Laodicea, every individual, family, race, region, city or nation has a redemptive gift lying within it. Coincidentally your dream/vision operates in perfect harmony with that redemptive gift. So the question for those who have visions to change their cities is, 'what is the redemptive gift in your region and how does your vision/dream enhance it'? This and many other questions need to be answered to operate in Quantum Leadership to it's fullest degree.

The Place Called There

If Quantum Leadership is the process of leading from the future, then the future revealed or aspired to must be clear and known. This is true for individuals, families, businesses and organizations. The place 'THERE' is THAT point in the future, it is the DESTINATION that needs to be reached. Many of the reasons people get stuck in life is because they don't have a clear view of the future. With our busy lives, seeing what 'THERE' looks like can be a challenge. Without clarity, 'THERE' can seem uncertain and result in inertia. I believe that the Father wants to use the 'FUTURE WITHIN' to change our world and needs you to employ quantum leadership to do so.

CHAPTER EIGHT

The Future Wars

This chapter is not one where I am predicting coming wars in the conventional sense. It is designed to engage you to fight for your dreams and fight for your future. The Apostle Paul is speaking to his spiritual son and encourages him to fight.

> This charge I commit unto thee, son Timothy, according to the prophecies which went before on thee, that thou by them mightest war a good warfare;
> **I Timothy 1:18**

Timothy is encouraged to wage war using the prophecies which he had received. I wasn't there at the time and could not tell you what was said under prophetic inspiration to him. One thing, I am sure of is that the content of the prophecies included insight into his future. As explained in a previous chapter, the dream-killer's assignment is activated and targeting the future of every human that has been born. As we delve into the realm of the invisible, we understand that our future was determined in Eternity before the foundations of the world, however our enemy in the second heaven has also planned a future for us. That future is designed to misuse our God-given talents and use them for his purposes. His mission for the future lying deep within you is to abort and throw it to the wayside. A future where our free will is used to harm others and produce evil in the Earth. There are so many examples of this in modern times as some of the evils we face include paedophile rings, slavery, criminal gangs, drug/sex trafficking, greed, radical Islam agenda and genocide etc. There are people and groups whose whole outlook for their future is dark and involves the suffering of the innocent. Just as there's a future inspired by the Father, there is also a Future that the enemy inspires, activates and uses our environment and life structures to enact them. He spends years analysing governments, businesses, families and individuals looking for portals of entry to disrupt and influence the future. You had better believe that these entities are planning a future that will affect you and I negatively.

For example, most businesses are targeting your disposable income and plan clever campaigns to get that money out of your pocket. The drug dealer sees a future where his/her clientele or territory increases and is either targeting you and your loved ones. Extreme fringe groups and globalists are lobbying western governments creating legislation and trade agreements that are threatening the very tenets of democracy. There are people and organizations that have an outlook of the future that is very different from ours; who are planning and creating a reality of the future according to what they can 'see'. The reason for mentioning the above is to welcome you to "the Future Wars". The Father sees all of this and wants to enlist you to join Him in partnership to create a brighter future. However, to accomplish this, He needs you to tap into your true-Life Dream so that He can bring it into fruition. Your Life Dream is His secret weapon to impact the world for Him and His Kingdom. When your light is never allowed to shine, it will make this world a darker place. The solution for some of our societal ills is lying deep within you and contained in your life dream. This is the main reason for any process or warfare you are experiencing right now; your dream/future is too powerful for the enemy to ignore.

In chapter four, we saw that the solution for Egypt's future problem was found in a teenaged boy living in Canaan. Father isn't waiting for a future problem to manifest, He plants the solution many years in advance in the form of a life dream. However, he is waiting for people like you and I to discover the realm of eternity within us, in order to turn the life dream into reality.

The Future Seen

As previously mentioned, the Apostle Paul essentially told Timothy to 'fight' for his future, by using the prophetic information received. The first principle for entering the future wars is 'seeing' a future worth fighting for. In other words, perceiving an aspect of the future while living in the present. Father loves to reveal and communicate, that's just the way He is and if that wasn't the case then the 'prophetic' wouldn't exist. He uses the prophetic to convey on most occasions, His thoughts on the present and the future. In fact, His language is more often in a present-future tense than anything else. By His Spirit, Father reveals the future and once revelation is revealed its ownership changes. Deuteronomy Chapter 29 verse 29 says something really powerful,

> "The secret things belong unto the Lord our God: but those
> things which are revealed belong unto us and to our children
> for ever, that we may do all the words of this law"

In other words, the things that remain unrevealed belongs to the Father, however once these 'things' are REVEALED, the ownership is transferred. One of those 'things' is our FUTURE and once it is uncovered it BELONGS to you. Once it is SEEN/REVEALED, that future belongs to you and you have the right to fight for it. My question to you is this, what does your future look like? Can you describe vividly what your revealed future looks like, or is it vague and opaque? Pastors, what does your city and congregation look like in the future? Business Leaders, what does your organization look like in the future? Take a moment, let your imagination soar and begin to describe things in higher definition.

Prophecy was never intended to solely affect your spirit; it was also designed to affect your mind and imagination. Words can create mental images. If I said to you, imagine a dark brown cat prowling on your roof. It has a black tip on its tail. Mental images are being formed. The prophetic works in a similar way, it creates mental images of the future that is designed to forever alter the world INSIDE you. Once seen in this dimension, the future has a pathway from the invisible to the visible into your present. It now becomes a reality within you, a scene or a destination to be reached and is now called 'THERE'. For 'THERE' to be created, it must simply become a permanent fixture in your prayer life and declarations. The language of faith must be used to reinforce the image within. 'THERE' must become the focal point of all the goals being set and the plans being formulated.

Life Dream Statement

'I will stand upon my watch, and set me upon the tower, and will watch to see what he will say unto me, and what I shall answer when I am reproved.

And the Lord answered me, and said, Write the vision, and make it plain upon tables, that he may run that readeth it.'

For the vision is yet for an appointed time, but at the end it shall speak, and not lie: though it tarry, wait for it; because it will surely come, it will not tarry.'
Habakkuk Chapter 2:1-3

The place called 'THERE' can be encapsulated in what I call a Life Dream Statement. It is a written description of what the revealed future looks like. This document is essential and will bring your future into focus. Armed with existing prophetic information and with the knowledge that 'eternity' resides within you, it is now time to take a prolonged LOOK at the future and CAPTURE it. The Life Dream statement is not just for individuals, but for families, churches, businesses and other organizations. It is literally a DREAM statement which incorporates all the nuances of your calling and places them in ONE document. Over time, this document will need to be revised. The reason is because revelation, prophetic information and our own understanding are progressive in nature. The closer we come to our future, the more DETAIL we will see.

The Place Called 'Here'

However, before this process begins an honest assessment of where 'HERE' is must be made. Looking at where 'HERE' is and seeing the vastness of 'THERE' or the BIGNESS of your life dream can be intimidating. As both places can appear incongruent. Be encouraged, when looking to form a nation that would exhibit His Light to the world, Father started with a couple that was infertile. At that time, the promise of the future (THERE) did not correlate with what Abram and Sarai were going through (HERE). That did not stop them from taking their first steps towards their journey to the future that would affect future generations. It is a challenge that all of us face living in these times. Can we step towards a future that will affect generations to come?? The place 'HERE' in some cases, could be in a place of brokenness, lack, hurt and disappointment.

If I have described your current situation, I want you to know something. God's grace SPECIALIZES in taking people from broken places into a future that He has designed for them. He isn't looking for perfection but for those who will run their race with endurance. He is looking for those although broken, hurt and disappointed who will allow His Grace to work through their issues as they step towards their life dream. The circumstances used to cause the pain can be a tool of the enemy to keep you trapped in a present clouded by the past to keep you in a perpetual orbit around the negative events in your life.

A practical application would be looking at where you are at the start of your journey. When analysing, 'HERE' understand that it is only the START of your journey and when viewed in context with your future can become the launchpad into something great and lifechanging. Remember the revealed future needs to be where you are aiming and at times can take many years to reach. 'Here' will also inform you of where you are in life, your status in terms of finances, relationships and resources available.

Don't allow the lack of resources to cause you to place your 'Dream' on the shelf. Learn to work with what you have. Be as resourceful and productive with your current budget and you'll see that your resources will increase to the level required over time. 'Here' also includes where 'you' are on your journey, physically, emotionally and spiritually. The decision to create your future will impact your whole life and those who are closely connected to you. After taking an inventory of 'Here' your eyes now need to be fixed on where you are going.

Diagram 5

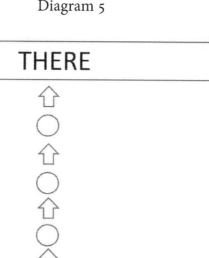

The diagram shows a clear starting point or a place where the journey recommences or begins. Between the places Here and There, are stepping stones and arrows. The stones represent the goals needed to get there and the arrows are the associated action plans. When setting the goals, an important principle to be used is 'that it is the destination that determines your decisions or progressive goal setting.' These goals have to be time-sensitive and realistic and have the END in view.

> Commit to the Lord whatever you do,
> and he will establish your plans.
> The Lord works out everything to its proper end—
> even the wicked for a day of disaster.
> **Proverbs 16:2-4**

Setting goals is a necessity but action is also needed.

> What good is it, my brothers and sisters, if someone claims
> to have faith but has no deeds? Can such faith save them?
> Suppose a brother or a sister is without clothes and daily
> food. If one of you says to them, "Go in peace; keep warm
> and well fed," but does nothing about their physical needs,
> what good is it? In the same way, faith by itself, if it is not
> accompanied by action, is dead.
> **James 2:14-17**

As previously stated, it is the destination that determines decisions.
'THERE' should shape the goals being set and in turn the goals being
set determine the content of the action plans. The journey towards
the future begins one step at a time. It should be noted that the
importance of involving the Holy Spirit is paramount. Remain open
to trusted prophetic voices and the leadership that have been placed
strategically in your life. This will keep you in line with the Lord's
continuous processes. Attempting to pursue your life dream in
isolation isn't wise and can lead to discouragement and deception.
To get 'THERE' will involve people and key relationships that
appear at divinely orchestrated moments on your journey. Why??
Because the journey to your future is not as linear as described in
the above diagram.

This is the reason why Timothy was encouraged to fight for his
future. Our enemy will use all he can to place obstacles, distractions
and hurdles in pursuit of our future. Life can at times throw
curveballs or throw you off course, but knowing 'Where' you are on
your journey to the place called 'There' is extremely important. The
following diagram is probably a more realistic outlook on what this
journey could look like:

Diagram 6

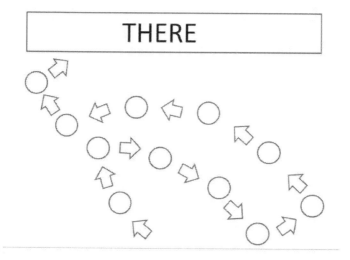

As you can see, there's a start, and then some setbacks or 'processing' occurs that may cause you to take a couple of steps backwards. Even if that is the case, remember you are not the same person that started the journey, you have grown and have more experience now. You are learning what works for you and the lessons that making mistakes can teach you. The place called 'Here' is constantly shifting as your journey continues whether or not certain goals are being not being accomplished. Regular appraisals and reflections are necessary tools in order to turn your dreams into reality. This journey WILL require patience and endurance. Whatever happens, keep your future or 'THERE' in focus.

The book of Hebrews, offers insight into the mentality needed:

> 'Therefore, since we are surrounded by such a great cloud of witnesses, let us throw off everything that hinders and the sin that so easily entangles. And let us run with perseverance the race marked out for us.'
> **Hebrews 12:1**

What the verse above reveals is that there is a race set before everyone. This race has a starting point and a finishing line. The starting is point relates to 'Here' and the finishing point corresponds with 'There'. If we use the Apostle Paul and the Lord Himself as examples, they both knew what their respective finishing lines where. Likewise, both had insight into their future and used it to press on despite the opposition that was present in their lives. Another related example is a young man who grew to become Israel's greatest King. He was the youngest of eight boys in a Judean family during the reign of King Saul. David was tasked by his father, Jesse to be a shepherd and look after the flock of sheep entrusted to him. One day out of nowhere, he gets a message to come to the family home during the visit of Samuel the Prophet. While he makes his way to the house, Samuel anoints him with oil and announces that David will be the next King of Israel. The prophetic in operation was outlining David's future and what 'THERE' looked like for him.

Soon after this powerful prophetic declaration, Israel wars with the Philistines but there's a problem, a new deadly threat has arrived in the form of the lethal warrior during that time. It was a giant whose name was Goliath who descended from the lineage of giants known as the Rephaim that mysteriously survived Joshua's previous purge generations before. With both armies in formation and directly opposite each other, a challenge is issued for Israel to find a champion that could fight and defeat Goliath. The Israeli soldiers are intimidated and afraid and looking to Saul who doesn't know what to do. He then requests volunteers who would dare to face this threat. For days the challenge is rehearsed with the Philistine army mocking their adversaries. David happens to be sending supplies to his brothers who were enlisted in the army and hears the challenge from the Goliath and the Philistine army. After asking what the reward would be for facing Goliath, David volunteers himself to face the giant.

Unknown to everyone, David had faced threats before. While defending his father's flock, he encountered firstly a lion and then a bear who threatened the flock. He killed them both. These were life-threatening situations but were also opportunities to grow and develop into a skillful warrior. It is important to note that in order to kill these ferocious animals, David had to have spent several hours practising with his slingshot. These opportunities were 'preparation' for the threats that he would indeed face in the 'future'. The skills honed while he was hidden in the wilderness looking after the family's sheep prepared him for this encounter with Goliath. As you keep this in mind, look at your present situations with a new perspective. Perhaps you are being 'future trained' like David was. Despite what you are facing right now, your circumstance has created an environment for you to GROW and to be trained for your future. The day of confrontation finally arrived and David faces his deadly adversary. Goliath has armour and the conventional weapons of warfare, including a sword and spear. Both combatants are skilled warriors but only ONE has insight into the future and operated in covenant relationship with the Living God. In the natural, there appears to be only one winner, the giant with many years of battle-hardened experience. However, in the realm of the

Spirit with the backing of the God of Heaven and the knowledge of his destiny, David emerges victorious. Understanding this principle will enable you to OUTLAST your storm KNOWING that you will, in time, enter a future that has been ORDAINED for you. Here's what the Apostle Paul said:

> Brethren, I count not myself to have apprehended: but this one thing I do, forgetting those things which are behind, and reaching forth unto those things which are before,
>
> I press toward the mark for the prize of the high calling of God in Christ Jesus.
> **Philippians 3:13-14**

These verses, in my humble opinion, describe a FutureNow mentality. It's a mindset of reaching forward for what's ahead instead of allowing the past and the present to restrict or imprison you. In athletics, especially in the sprinting events, athletes are trained to dip or lean in as they approach the finish line. Failure to do so could cost the athlete the race. With this in mind, please 'open' your eyes again and LOOK at the finishing line; the place called 'THERE' that the Father has revealed to you. It is that PLACE, DREAM or 'VISION that we all should be intentionally reaching and pressing towards. Your past and present situation or circumstances will not be able to contain you once your eyes are FOCUSED on a future reality situated beyond your present one.

CHAPTER NINE

A Time for Game Changers

At the beginning of this book, I noted some game-changers that adjusted the course of history. There have been remarkable men and women who have contributed to creating a brighter future in their day. For me, the ultimate gamechanger is none other than the Lord Jesus Christ, who in His short life, changed the world forever. His divine Lifestyle invited the Future to touch the World in such a powerful and dramatic way. This Man continues to move in the lives of people throughout the Earth, inviting them to do likewise in their sphere of influence. We live in a time, where more game-changers are needed from every walk of life and in every nation. Beloved, I am believing God that whoever is reading this book right now, is having the future within stirring you to ACTION.

Are you a game-changer our world needs right now??

An Uncertain Sound

Our problem today in the church is that we are focusing on the wrong part of the pending future. This has resulted in a malaise, causing us to become inactive in influencing our culture and society. It is definitely not the design from the Lord and His ministry. We focus on living in Heaven for eternity but the scriptures reveal the Father's ultimate objective is getting Heaven on Earth. If your future is based on just passing through just to get to heaven, there really is no need to mobilize efforts to transform our communities and culture into what Heaven desires them to be. If our attention is on the coming Anti-Christ and his emergence, then again, we are missing the point. There's a danger that we'll become too fatalistic while waiting for the inevitable transition for the worst. Many 'prophetic' conferences are based on 'pre or post tribulation eschatology, which I feel needs to revisited with fresh eyes. Most believers when asked about the future of the church either point to heaven or the emerging systems of the Anti-Christ. Let me put this into perspective. The coming AntiChrist has two periods of three-and-a-half years to govern the future world government. However, the next major leader, Jesus, the Messiah is due to reign for at least 1,000 years from the City of Jerusalem. For centuries, Satan has planned for a one world government but his tenure is coming to an end. Jesus Himself IS the focal point of the future.

A prophetic voice can at times be likened to a trumpet. While in the wilderness during Moses' time, the Israeli's were trained to hear certain trumpet blasts which would mean certain things. However, if the trumpet gave an uncertain sound, the people wouldn't know what to do. This is a problem within prophetic communities today; the 'Sound' being released is uncertain, meaning the people are unable to discern the times in which they live in order to strategize the future. In 2016, during the last American election, I actually heard leading prophetic voices declaring that both Hilary Clinton and Donald Trump would win. How can you strategize for the future when the sound is uncertain?? Those prophecies actually came down to, in some cases, the ethnicity of the prophet and his or her political persuasion. Meanwhile, various movements are planning 25 to 30 years in the future, with pristine clarity, on how they want to shape culture and the future. In the West due to recent cultural lifestyle choices the birth rate amongst the indigenous is falling due to abortion and 'lifestyle' changes whilst the birth rate amongst legal and illegal immigrants continues to rise. This is one of the reasons why immigration is one of the hot topics of our day, as shrewd people groups on both sides of the argument are looking at the future. Demographics are changing and clever movements, businesses, politicians are waiting to take advantage. These movements are already planning for a tomorrow when their numbers increase to such a level that they can influence the nations in which they currently live. The levers of power remain the same, hence, determining whoever pulls them starts today.

Kingdom Origins

Adam's first sin established a future culminating in the events described in the book of Revelation. This book outlines how the kingdoms/systems of this world eventually become the Kingdoms of our Lord and of His Christ. When the Earth was originally created, it was in harmony with Heaven and the Kingdom was extended into the visible world through it's King, Adam. Adam was both created and made, his spirit first before being housed in a body and becoming a living soul.

> What is man, that thou art mindful of him? and the son of man, that thou visitest him?
>
> For thou hast made him a little lower than the angels, and hast crowned him with glory and honour.
>
> Thou madest him to have dominion over the works of thy hands; thou hast put all things under his feet:
> Psalms 8:4-6

The above referenced text describes Adam being crowned with glory. He was crowned King and was a physical representation of the Kingdom of Heaven on Earth. According to the book of Genesis, Adam switched allegiences with an outlawed supernatural entity called Satan/Lucifer. Adam and his wife ate from the tree of the knowledge of good and evil which resulted in their eyes being opened to 'see' things they were never intended to see. Instantaneously, the world and nature itself was changed for the worst, resulting in the introduction of evil into our world. Murder, wars, sickness, disease, poverty, oppressive regimes and systems were the consequence. Through his insidious intervention, Satan became the 'god of this world'. Thousands of years later whilst tempting Jesus in the wilderness, Satan himself reveals the following:

> And the devil, taking him up into an high mountain, shewed unto him all the kingdoms of the world in a moment of time.

> And the devil said unto him, All this power will I give thee, and the glory of them: for that is delivered unto me; and to whomsoever I will I give it.

> If thou therefore wilt worship me, all shall be thine.
> Luke 4:5-7

By being 'the god of this world' he became the 'god' of the world and it's systems. Satan said all the kingdoms/systems of this world were handed over to him, by whom?? The first Kings and rulers of Earth; Adam and Eve. When Adam fell, the systems also fell under satanic control. If that is the case, then it is not necessarily the systems of our world that are at fault, instead it is the people and their ideology governing or influencing these systems that matter. Jesus called

Himself the 'Light of the world'. The word 'world' is translated as 'kosmos' which indicates the people and the systems or arrangements in our world. It is the same 'world' that He came to save.

> For God so loved the world, that he gave his only begotten Son, that whosoever believeth in him should not perish, but have everlasting life.
>
> For God sent not his Son into the world to condemn the world; but that the world through him might be saved.
> **John 3:16-17**

The word "save" is defined as "salvaging or restoring to its original form or intent". We need to understand that Father wants to restore not replace these systems. The Apostle Peter refers to this as he was reaching in Jerusalem soon after Jesus' resurrection:

> 'Repent, then, and turn to God, so that your sins may be wiped out, that times of refreshing may come from the Lord, 20 and that he may send the Messiah, who has been appointed for you—even Jesus. 21 Heaven must receive him until the time comes for God to restore everything, as he promised long ago through his holy prophets.'
> **Acts 3:19-21**

Since restoration means to bring it back to the point of origin, Adam's fall also resulted in a fallen system that needed to be salvaged or saved. Consequently, this would suggests that as a church, we must broaden our scope on what we are called to influence. According to Lance Wallnau, there are seven mountains or spheres of influence in a society:

Family

The traditional family unit is the foundation or building block of a functional society. Empirical data continues to show a correlation between crime, teenage pregnancies and other dysfunctional behaviour to the breakdown of the family unit. The statistics show that marriage and the traditional family is a source of spiritual, emotional and financial wellbeing for all. In the current climate of political correctness this data is being largely ignored. Our societies can be rebuilt with a focus to support and empower families and reverse the damage done by the rise of liberal and progressive ideas and lifestyles.

Religion

In every nation and society there is a belief system in a supernatural God or gods depending on where you are on the Earth. For example, Hinduism, Islam, Buddhism, Christianity and Judasim etc. These belief systems in most cases are the bedrock of the values in that particular nation.

Arts and Entertainment

Arts and entertainment play a huge part in every nation and society. The values, behaviour and cultural tastes are in many ways influenced by the arts and entertainment industry. There can be no doubt that the sustained debasing of the arts and entertainment industry has contributed to the recent changes in our society.

Media

The media in it's varied forms is a megaphone for whoever controls it. It's ability to sway the public's opinion is second to none. Newspapers, Television, Blogs, Youtube etc are able to inseminate information to the populace in a way that none other can. This is the reason why businesses, organisations and politicians pay handsomely for 'airtime in order to influence the populace with their products, services and ideas. In recent times 'fake news' has become a problem as established media giants are becoming polarised in their political views and have become increasingly biased.

Business/Finance

The ability to create wealth is integral to every nation. The economic wellbeing of any nation is in many ways determined by those who operate in trading products and services. From the self employed individual or small businesses to large corporations. The markets and economic systems that have emerged are vitally important. However, the values that govern these markets and systems are also equally important. Greed, corruption and price fixing amongst so called competitors have caused widespread problems in the past. Economic power has incredible leverage in our day and can and often does influence local and national governments.

Education

Education has the ability to shape the thinking of the young and next generation. It has also been traditionally used to prepare the young for the world of work. However, in recent times the education system in the West has been politicized and hijacked by movements that are actively working to either revise history or propagate their agenda. In history, especially in the 20th century, we have seen the education system used for propaganda purposes to support totalitarian regimes formed by Hitler and Stalin.

Government

Politics refers to a set of activities associated with the governance of a country, or an area. It involves making decisions that apply to members of a group. It refers to achieving and exercising positions of governance—organized control over a human community, particularly a state. In history, political power has been wielded by a variety of governing institutions ie a monarchy, a republic, a parliamentary democracy etc. Whatever the form of government the most important aspect is the underlying ideology of a person or a political party that operates in government. It is the ideology that often determines the legislative decisions that can affect every one of the previously mention spheres of influence.

The Call To Action

These spheres operate in every nation and shapes the culture within them. If the culture or society is changed, then the future of a nation is changed also. The Gospel of the Kingdom and its directives dictate that we go into all the world and share this lifechanging message and the ideology that compliments it. This isn't just a geographical assignment but a universal directive to enter and influence major spheres of influence. The future stirring within you is destined to influence one or some of these mountains.

Our problem in the West is that we have allowed other ideologies to incrementally bend and shape our culture into what it has become today. Political correctness is nothing more than a Marxist/socialist tool designed to negatively transform a society. Related people/movements have targeted these spheres for decades and now dictate the agenda in politics, media and in education. This didn't happen overnight or by osmosis, but with careful implementation of plans that were concocted many years ago.

The church has retreated from these other mountain/spheres to operate in the religious mountain, thinking that we can bring change from this mountain alone. The prayers for revival, the prophetic, glory meetings are good and necessary for awakening, but are simply not enough for REFORMATION. Previous generations of Christians understood the challenge to bring and be a LIGHT. Organizations and movements were formed to address the evil and injustice in their day. A lot of the rights and freedoms we take for granted today were fought by previous generations. For example, the abolitionist and civil rights movements were birthed in the church and changed their respective countries for the better. The truth is that existing systems are failing, people are suffering, YOUR call and assignment CAN and WILL make a difference. If your dream is on the shelf, blow the dust off and try again for these are days for dreams to be FULFILLED.

The good news is that the Father is never caught by surprise and has been planning His response from the beginning of time. You and the FUTURE placed within you are part of His plan to increase a divine influence into our society. I believe that we are being set up for something quite extraordinary and unprecedented. Gamechangers are going to arise from unusual places doing unusual things within these spheres of influence. Being strategically positioned and commissioned to maximize the influence of His Kingdom with the mandate to transform society from WITHIN is imperative. The FUTURE within you addresses the evil in our day and brings solutions, ideas and systems that will enact change in every sphere of society.

Are you ready to be the gamechanger our world needs right now? Are you ready to be the portal or doorway to a brighter future?

If that's the case, then it is time to live a lifestyle that brings the ultimate FUTURENOW reality, the Kingdom of our King to transform our lives, our community, city, nation and culture.

It is now time to live the FUTURE NOW.

About The Author

Otis Pinnock is a prophetic voice based in Milton Keynes, United Kingdom. He is an Entrepreneur, Author and Broadcaster. He is also the Founder and Senior Leader of EmpowerU Network, a Kingdom Based movement that seeks to bring transformation to individuals, couples, families, cities, regions and nations. Since 1989 he has had a variety of church leadership roles and has been a key itinerant speaker in churches/conferences extensively in the UK, USA and Canada. He operates under an unusual prophetic anointing that facilitates breakthrough. His passion for empowerment and transformation has also taken him to the Caribbean and Africa.

Otis has over 24 years of experience in business providing care services for Adults with Learning Disabilities in North West London. He serves currently as the Managing Director of Empower Community Care an organisation dedicated to community care for the vulnerable.

Otis teaches and releases POTENTIAL. He believes there is a life to live without limits once potential has been identified. To book him for speaking engagements or for any of the programs he offers please use the details below to contact our office.

www.Otispinnock.com
Email: op@otispinnock.com
Tel: +44 1908 766287

The Future Now is the first of many books that we intend to publish. To be notified of any new publications why not join our mailing list by using the details below.

www.empowerpublishing.net

Thank you.

Endnotes

https://www.hebrew4christians.com/Holidays/Introduction/introduction.html

https://www.bible-history.com/biblestudy/caesarea-philippi.html

Made in the USA
Columbia, SC
11 August 2020